Recipes from My Mother

This book is dedicated to the two mothers in my life. To my mum Hallfridur, who is loving and wise in every situation, and has given me the best start in life. And to my dynamic, indefatigable mother-in-law Darina, who has dedicated her life to teaching and inspiring future generations to feed themselves and others in the best possible way. Thank you both.

HarperCollins*Publishers*
1 London Bridge Street,
London, SE1 9GF

www.harpercollins.co.uk

First published by HarperCollins*Publishers* 2017

10 9 8 7 6 5 4 3 2 1

A catalogue record of this book is available from the British Library.

ISBN: 978-0-00-820817-2

Food styling: Annie Rigg
Prop styling: Lydia Brun

Printed and bound in Spain

MIX
Paper from
responsible sources
FSC™ C007454

FSC™ is a non-profit international organisation established to promote the responsible management of the world's forests. Products carrying the FSC label are independently certified to assure consumers that they come from forests that are managed to meet the social, economic and ecological needs of present and future generations, and other controlled sources.

Find out more about HarperCollins and the environment at
www.harpercollins.co.uk/green

RACHEL ALLEN

Recipes from My Mother

Delicious recipes filled with memories

 HarperCollins*Publishers*

CONTENTS

INTRODUCTION

I've always been fascinated by what makes people the way they are. We are like very complex, colourful tapestries, and as with every other living being, no two of us are exactly the same. We are all, of course, a product of two different people, but who we are as actual individuals goes deeper and is much more interesting than that. The place where we grew up, the climate, the cultures, the traditions and, not least, the food we eat all play a part in weaving together the fibres that make us who we are.

I grew up in Dublin with a sister, an Irish father and a mother from Iceland. I've always been very proud of my half-Icelandic and half-Irish heritage. I count myself fortunate in that it was a very happy home with lots of good food. While my father made great brown bread and the best poached eggs in town, it was my mum who always cooked a delicious and nutritious meal for us all to eat at the end of the day. She had first one, then two, busy boutiques (while even whipping up the clothes for the shop herself on the sewing machine in the 1970s) and somehow there was always a great meal ready for us in the evening.

My favourites were the kinds of dishes that many people call comfort food – roast chicken, stews and casseroles – for which there is rarely a traditional Irish recipe as every family has their own. Despite only arriving in Dublin when she was 19, my mother seemed to quickly master the Irish flavours and cooking techniques. Recipes such as St Patrick's Day Bacon with Parsley Sauce and Cabbage Purée (page 129) and Irish Stew with Pearl Barley (page 136) were a regular feature of my childhood. Looking back on it now, I am so appreciative of the fact that I got to sit down at the table to enjoy these meals with my family and catch up on what had happened during the day. It's the one thing that my husband, Isaac, and I insist on now with our children – for me it's one of the most important times of the day.

I'm also very appreciative of the fact that as a child, family holidays often took us abroad. By visiting different countries, I was introduced to a wealth of different foods and flavours. So it felt right to include a few dishes inspired by these memories – Mussels with Tomato, Chorizo, Sherry and Parsley (page 156), for example, and Tomato Risotto with Lemon and Basil Mascarpone (page 170).

Although my mother has lived in Dublin since marrying my father, she grew up in Iceland. Life in Reykjavik in the 1940s was, of course, very different from what it is now. Mum and her family lived close to the docks, which was where they would go to get their just-caught fish and also smoked fish, which was prepared as soon as it came in from the boats and was very popular because nobody had fridges. Being an island nation with not a huge amount of vegetation, fish featured a lot in their diet, much more so than meat, though if there was meat it was lamb. Even with a mainly fish diet, my mum remembers that children were all given cod liver oil in school every day as a supplement!

One of my favourite Icelandic foods that Mum often used to eat and we enjoyed on holidays in Iceland is *harðfiskur* – the salted dried fish. I can still remember we used to eat it cold, spread with salted butter, as did Mum when she was young. It's still really popular there and although it's more often eaten as a snack, it is sometimes heated in soups and stews. I tried to make it recently at home in County Cork, but it just didn't match up to the authentic Icelandic version, which is dried in the North Atlantic sea breeze. I guess I'll just have to wait for my next trip to Iceland until I have some more. Breakfast for my mum before she would skate across the Tjörnin lake in the middle of Reykjavik to get to school in wintertime was a bowl of *skyr*, which is a bit like a Greek yoghurt, but is technically a cheese (as described on page 15). Mum remembers it being incredibly thick in the tub, so it would be thinned out with milk. In the wintertime it was scattered with cinnamon sugar and during the long, bright summers, they would enjoy it with berries. These were mainly blueberries that they'd picked at the weekend when visiting their relatives in the countryside, where they would also go camping, ride ponies and, in the wintertime, ski. The dairy where they used to buy *skyr* was next door to the bakery where my mum's favourite treat of all came from – *vinabroð*. These are gorgeous little delicacies made with puff pastry

and an almond or custard topping, and Mum still remembers how they were always wrapped in baking parchment for her and her little sister to bring back home. One of the most popular Icelandic pastries still is *kleinur*, but Mum remembers these were more often than not made at home, as being deep-fried they need to be eaten as soon as they're made. My *amma* (Icelandic for grandmother – my mum's mum) used to make these for Grandpa, as he adored them, like my children do now. Unfortunately I never got Amma's *kleinur* recipe from her, but my version, which is on page 222, hopefully does justice to hers.

I get such pleasure when I see my children enjoying really good food, whether it's fish that they've caught, filleted and cooked themselves, shrimps that my daughter learnt how to peel and demolish by the dozen from her great-grandmother, or the seeds that they've planted and watched turn into sweet, crunchy carrots or cucumbers. I hope that they'll get the opportunity to teach and inspire future generations, passing on the appreciation and joy that there is to be had from great food.

As well as chatting to my own mum about the food that she loved as a child, I've been lucky enough to get wonderful stories and recipes from some of my friends, and indeed my mother-in-law Darina, about the food that was cooked for them by their mothers.

Thanks to all my friends who offered not only recipes but inspiration too: from Patricia for her tales of weekly liver with onions; Helen with her mother's delicious apple cake recipe, which I've tweaked to feature plums (page 190); Nessa, whose mother Margaret lent me her precious three-generation-old handwritten cookbook; Fingal and his mum Giana for the wonderful stories and many emails; and Pam for the lovely tip of using breadcrumbs in a crumble like her mum Sheila did and still does. Thanks to Ted and his mum Charlotte for the delicious Swedish seed crackers recipe, to Lara for many wonderful stories about her childhood and her love of food in Iceland, and to Jasper, Tiffany and their mum Julia, who so generously gave me more wonderful recipes than I had space for.

I hope that you too enjoy the recipes in this book and feel inspired to pass them down to the next generation.

Rachel

Breakfasts

(From left to right) Amma, my great-grandfather, and my great-Amma.

Skyr

Skyr is one of the Icelandic tastes of my childhood. Otherwise known as Icelandic curds, *skyr* is an age-old recipe dating back to the ninth century. It's often compared to Greek yoghurt, but strictly speaking it is a cheese – thicker than yoghurt with a slight cheesy tang. It's delicious, and is sometimes served with a little cream and brown sugar or, as I remember it, a splash of milk and a sprinkle of sugar. My sister and I used to have milk and sugar over natural yoghurt at home in Dublin to try to replicate the flavour. Making your own *skyr* is not unlike making yoghurt, although often a couple of drops of rennet are added and the 'set' milk is cut and strained to release the whey from the curds. *Skyr* can be left plain or flavoured with honey, coffee, vanilla and even herbs such as mint, rosemary and thyme. Homemade *skyr* will keep, covered, in the fridge for one week.

1 litre (1¾ pints) full-cream milk (I like to use an organic unpasteurised milk if possible, but other milk can be used)

1 tbsp skyr, from a previous batch if possible or shop bought (failing that, use a live active culture yoghurt)

2 drops of rennet or vegetable rennet (optional)

1. Place the milk in a saucepan over a very low heat and warm it slowly until it reaches 90°C (195°F). This should take 1 hour. Take it off the heat and set aside, at room temperature, to cool until it reaches 40°C (105°C) – 30 minutes. If this step is done too quickly, it could affect the setting of the skyr.

2. Add 1 tablespoon skyr (or yoghurt) and whisk to combine, making sure not to scrape the bottom of the pot. Next, stir in the rennet, if using. Place a lid on the saucepan and wrap it with two tea towels, then leave to stand at room temperature for 12–15 hours (a few more hours will probably be ok if you have to leave the house, but definitely not more than 24 hours).

3. By this stage, the milk should have thickened and you should notice the see-through whey separating from the brilliant white curds. Place a clean piece of muslin or cheesecloth in a sieve set over a bowl. Using a clean knife, cut the curds into a grid-shape, then tip into the lined sieve. Tie the material into a knot or tie with string, then hang the bundle from a hook or a wooden spoon stuck through the knot and suspend it over the bowl, removing the sieve. The fabric should not be touching the whey that's dripping off it into the bowl. If your kitchen is quite warm, hang the skyr in the fridge.

4. Leave to hang for 2 hours or until the mixture in the bundle is quite thick and almost beginning to dry at the edges. If it's too dry, whisk in some of the whey to thin it out. It should be thicker than Greek yoghurt, but not as thick as cream cheese. Once it's thick enough, it can be eaten straight away or covered (flavoured or not) and placed in the fridge for up to a week. You can drink the nutrition-packed whey if you like.

Crunchy granola

MAKES ABOUT 1.5KG (3LB 5OZ) GRANOLA

A deliciously crunchy, nutty start to the day. Make this recipe your own by adding your favourite seeds, nuts or dried fruit.

125g (4½oz) butter or coconut oil

150ml (5fl oz) honey or maple or agave syrup

1 tsp vanilla extract

500g (1lb 2oz) oat flakes

100g (3½oz) almonds (preferably with with skin), coarsely chopped

100g (3½oz) chopped hazelnuts

100g (3½oz) desiccated coconut

100g (3½oz) pumpkin or hemp seeds

100g (3½oz) sunflower seeds

300g (11oz) dried fruit (such as chopped dried dates, figs, apricots, raisins or sultanas – I like a mixture)

1 tsp ground cinnamon

1. Preheat the oven to 170°C (325°F), Gas mark 3. Place the butter or coconut oil, the honey or syrup and the vanilla extract in a small saucepan and put on the heat to melt together.

2. Next, place the oat flakes, almonds, hazelnuts, desiccated coconut, pumpkin or hemp seeds and the sunflower seeds in a large bowl and mix. Add the melted butter (or coconut oil) and syrup mixture and stir really well to make sure it's evenly combined.

3. Spread the mixture out in a large roasting tin, lined with baking parchment, if you like (but it's not essential), and bake in the oven for 25 minutes or until the nuts and grains are a light golden brown. Stir the granola every 5 minutes so that it browns evenly in the oven.

4. Once brown, remove the granola from the oven and leave in the tray to cool, again stirring every now and then, scraping it from the bottom of the tray. If you transfer it into a bowl while it's warm, it will go soggy.

5. When it has cooled down, mix in the dried fruit and cinnamon. Transfer to an airtight container and store at room temperature. It will keep well for up to one month.

How to make butter and buttermilk

MAKES ABOUT 225G (8OZ) BUTTER

If you've ever over-whipped cream, you've been on your way to making butter. We make butter every day at the Ballymaloe cookery school and people are often really surprised at how easy it is. You can flavour it how you like, too – with herbs, spices or seaweed.

1 litre (1¾ pints) regular or double cream
2 pinches of sea salt, or dairy salt (if you can get it)
your favourite flavourings – chopped herbs, garlic, dried seaweed, icing sugar or spices (optional)

1. Pour the cream into the bowl of a food mixer and, using the whisk, whip the cream for 5–10 minutes on a medium-high speed (but not so high that it splashes everywhere) until it starts to split (as if you've over-beaten it). Continue to beat until the yellow fat separates from the buttermilk (you can use this buttermilk for baking). It will look completely scrambled.

2. Sit a sieve over a large, clean bowl. Place a double layer of muslin in the sieve – you'll need it to be larger than the sieve as you want to be able to gather up the edges – then pour the contents of the food mixer bowl into it. With the muslin still in the sieve, bring up the edges and squeeze really hard to remove all the buttermilk. When all the buttermilk has been squeezed out, place the butter that remains in the muslin in a bowl and wash well in cold water, squeezing it well to remove every last bit of buttermilk. If you don't do this the butter will go rancid after a couple of days.

3. Now pat the butter dry with kitchen paper, put it into a bowl and mix in the salt and any other flavourings you like, such as chopped herbs, garlic, dried seaweed, or even icing sugar and spice for melting over pancakes.

4. Shape the butter into a sausage shape by rolling it up in baking parchment, or into a rectangle, or whatever shape you like. You can also place it in a mould that you've lined with muslin, if you have one. When you're happy with the flavour and the shape of your butter, place it in the fridge until needed. It will keep for 10–12 days if you've washed it free of all the buttermilk.

How to make yoghurt

Yoghurt is fun and easy to make and allows you to flavour it how you like. I love the unsweetened tang and slightly irregular texture that comes from a homemade version.

1 litre (1¾ pints) full-cream milk
25g (1oz) skimmed milk powder
1 tbsp natural yoghurt, live active culture yoghurt will work best (see tip)

1. Pour the milk into a saucepan and set on a gentle heat. As the milk begins to warm up, add the milk powder and stir to dissolve. Heat the milk until it reads 90°C (194°F) on a cooking thermometer. (If judging by eye, the milk will be sweet-smelling and just coming to the boil – steaming and starting to froth around the edges.) Remove from the heat and leave to stand and cool for 30 minutes or until it reads 40°C (104°F) on the thermometer (or the milk has stopped steaming and feels just tepid when you dip your finger in and leave it there for a few seconds).

2. Stir in the yoghurt, cover the pan with a clean tea towel and leave in a warm place (or in a flask) until the mixture thickens – which will take 4–5 hours.

3. After this time, remove the tea towel and transfer the yoghurt to a jar or bowl, then cover and place in the fridge overnight.

TIP
For your next batch of yoghurt you can use 1 tablespoon of this homemade yoghurt instead of the shop-bought yoghurt.

Scrambled eggs back in the shell

SERVES 1

This is a cute way to give scrambled eggs to little ones. I think the best scrambled eggs are cooked slowly over a low heat until almost set but still creamy, then taken out of the pan straight away to avoid overcooking.

1–2 eggs, as preferred
1 tsp regular or double cream
a little knob of butter
sea salt and freshly ground black pepper

To serve
hot buttered toast

1. Using either an egg topper or a little knife or spoon, carefully open the egg at the top as you would a boiled egg. Pour the egg into a saucepan and add the cream and butter, season with salt and pepper and beat well with a fork or whisk. Place the empty eggshell in an eggcup (see tip).

2. Scramble the egg over a low heat, stirring all the time. When the egg is just cooked but still soft and a bit runny, spoon it carefully back into the eggshell. Serve with a teaspoon and lots of hot buttered toast.

TIP
You can rinse the eggshell and dry it in the oven, if you wish. Place it, cut side down, on kitchen paper in a very cool oven, preheated to 100°C (212°F), Gas mark ¼ for 10 minutes.

Sweet eggy bread

SERVES 4

Sweet, comforting and completely delicious, one taste of this brings me back to my childhood in an instant.

2 large eggs
4 tbsp regular or double cream
1–2 tbsp caster sugar, to taste
1 tsp vanilla extract or ½ tsp ground cinnamon
a little pinch of sea salt
50g (2oz) butter
4 large slices of white, wholemeal or sourdough bread

To serve
maple syrup, crispy bacon slices or icing sugar

1. In a bowl large enough to dip slices of bread into, whisk the eggs, cream, sugar and vanilla extract or cinnamon powder together with a pinch of salt.

2. Melt a knob of the butter in a frying pan over a medium-high heat until foaming. Dip both sides of a slice of bread into the egg mixture and then fry on both sides, adding more butter as needed, until golden. Keep warm in a low oven while you repeat with the remaining bread.

3. Repeat until all the slices of bread are fried. Serve drizzled with maple syrup and slices of crispy bacon or dusted with icing sugar.

Buckwheat crêpes with ham, cheese and eggs

SERVES 6

I love the nuttiness (and added nutrition) that buckwheat flour brings to these crêpes. This makes for a superb brunch or supper.

For the batter
100g (3½oz) buckwheat flour
½ tsp sea salt
1 egg
200ml (7fl oz) milk
40g (1½oz) butter, melted

For the filling
200g (7oz) Gruyère, Emmental or Comté cheese, grated
6 slices of best-quality ham
a little butter, for frying
6 eggs
sea salt and freshly ground black pepper

1. First, make the batter. Mix the flour and salt together in a bowl. Put the egg, milk and melted butter into a measuring jug, add 100ml (3½fl oz) water and whisk. Make a well in the centre of the dry ingredients, then pour the liquid into the well, whisking all the time to gradually draw in the flour from the edges of the bowl, until you have a smooth batter with a few bubbles on top. Use straight away, or it can store in the fridge for up to 24 hours.

2. Preheat the grill to medium or the oven to 200°C (400°F), Gas mark 6 (see tip).

3. Heat a frying pan (ovenproof if you're using the oven). Rub a piece of kitchen paper in the butter and wipe it over the base of the pan – do this each time you put in a new batch of batter. Pour in some of the batter and swirl it around to coat the base of the pan with a thin layer. Allow to fry until it sets and is golden underneath, then flip it over and immediately place a slice of ham in the centre of the crêpe. Cover the ham with grated cheese, leaving a little dip in the middle, and break the egg into the dip. Fold up the edges of the pancake to meet the edge of the egg white, then place the pan under the grill or in the oven until the cheese has melted and the egg is cooked. Repeat for all the other crêpes, serving each finished one at once.

TIP
You can either make all the crêpes first then fill and bake them one at a time, or if you have two pans and a bit of nerve, you can leave one pan cooking the finished crêpe in the oven while the other is cooking the batter on the hob.

Potato pancakes with black pudding and glazed apples

MAKES 12 PANCAKES

A great way to use up leftover potatoes, these little pancakes are almost blini-like and I adore the meaty black pudding and sweet, sticky glazed apple topping. Another great topping for these pancakes is the Beetroot, Dill and Horseradish Gravlax with Mustard and Dill Mayonnaise on page 80.

For the pancakes
75g (3oz) plain flour
½ tsp baking powder
½ tsp sea salt
2 eggs
125ml (4½fl oz) milk
225g (8oz) cold mashed
   potato (no butter or milk
   added)
15g (½oz) butter, for frying

For the glazed apples
40g (1½oz) butter
2 eating apples, peeled,
   quartered, cored and cut
   into 5mm (¼in) slices
30g (1¼oz) caster sugar
juice of ½ lemon

For the sage butter
50g (2oz) butter
2 tsp chopped sage

For the black pudding
15g (½oz) butter
about 24 slices (cut
   7.5mm/⅜in thick) black
   pudding (2 per pancake)
   – peel the skin off the
   black pudding before
   slicing

1. First, make the pancakes. Sift the flour and baking powder into a bowl, add the salt and mix. Crack the eggs into another bowl and whisk, then mix in the milk and mashed potato. Pour this into the dry ingredients, whisking as you add it. Set aside.

2. Heat a pan over a medium heat. Rub a piece of kitchen paper in the butter and wipe it over the base of the pan – do this each time you put in a new batch of batter. When the pan is hot, drop generous tablespoonfuls of the batter, spaced apart, in the pan. Cook for 2 minutes until golden underneath, then turn over and cook the other side until golden. Remove from the pan and keep them warm while you make the others.

3. Meanwhile, place a pan (another frying pan if you have one) over a medium-high heat and add the butter for the glazed apples. Allow it to melt and foam, then tip in the apple slices and spread them out. Toss them over the heat for a few minutes until they are light golden, then add the sugar and lemon juice and continue to toss until the apples are tender and beautifully glazed. Keep warm.

4. In a small saucepan, melt the butter for the sage butter and add the sage. Allow it to foam, then take the pan off the heat.

5. To cook the black pudding slices, place a frying pan over a medium-high heat and add the butter. Add the black pudding slices and fry until they are cooked on both sides and hot inside.

6. Divide the warm pancakes among warm plates. Top each pancake with a few glazed apple slices, then 2 slices of black pudding and, finally, a drizzle of hot sage butter.

Cheese and bacon muffins

MAKES 12 MUFFINS

These great savoury muffins are just crying out to be packed up and taken on a picnic.
I often use a mixture of leftover delicious farmhouse cheeses in these, which ensures
they're slightly different every time I make them.

150g (5oz) streaky bacon
    rashers
225g (8oz) plain flour
2 tsp baking powder
1 tbsp caster sugar
1 tsp sea salt
pinch of freshly ground
    black pepper
125g (4½oz) cheese, grated
    (I like a mixture of
    Cheddar, Gruyère and
    Parmesan)
1 egg
75g (3oz) butter, melted
225ml (8fl oz) milk
1 tsp Dijon mustard

1. Preheat the oven to 190°C (375°F), Gas mark 5. Line a 12-cup muffin tray
   with 12 paper cases.

2. Cook the bacon rashers in a frying pan over a medium heat until golden and
   crisp on both sides. Chop into pieces 1cm (½in) in size.

3. Sift the flour and the baking powder into a bowl. Add the sugar, salt
   and pepper, then mix in the grated cheese and crisp bacon pieces. Whisk
   the egg in another bowl and mix in the melted butter, the milk and the
   mustard. Make a well in the centre of the dry ingredients and stir in the wet
   ingredients until combined.

4. Divide the mixture among the 12 paper cases and bake in the oven for
   20–25 minutes until golden and a skewer comes out clean from the centre
   of a muffin. Transfer to a wire rack to cool.

Banana pancakes

MAKES ABOUT 12 PANCAKES

Our boys loved these when they were little, and they still love them now. The bananas are great for adding natural sweetness and, of course, nutrition-packed goodness, too.

150g (5oz) plain flour
1 tsp baking powder
¼ tsp bread soda
   (bicarbonate of soda)
1 tbsp caster sugar (optional)
2 eggs
150ml (5fl oz) buttermilk
25g (1oz) butter, melted
1 large or 1½ medium
   bananas, peeled and
   mashed just before using
a few knobs of butter
butter or maple syrup, to
   serve

1. Sift the flour, baking powder and bread soda into a bowl. Add the caster sugar (if using) and stir to mix.

2. Crack the eggs into another bowl and whisk, then stir in the buttermilk and melted butter. Make a well in the centre of the dry ingredients and pour the liquid into the dry ingredients, whisking as you add it. The batter is ready to use or can be stored in the fridge overnight.

3. Just before you want to cook the pancakes, fold the mashed bananas into the batter.

4. Heat a large frying pan over a medium heat and melt a couple of knobs of butter, making sure the base of the pan is covered with a thin layer of butter. I normally wipe the butter all over the pan with some kitchen paper, which I'll use to re-butter the pan for each batch of pancakes.

5. Drop large spoonfuls (about 50ml/2fl oz each) of the pancake batter into the hot pan – leave plenty of space between them as the pancakes spread while cooking. Turn the heat down slightly or the pancakes will burn before they're cooked in the centre. You should be able to fit four or five in the pan at a time. Cook on the first side until bubbles appear and pop on the upper surface – 1–2 minutes – then, using a fish slice or something similar, turn the pancakes over and finish cooking on the other side for another minute or so until golden brown. Cook all the pancakes in this way in a few batches, keeping the cooked ones warm in a low oven until they are all ready. Serve with butter or maple syrup – or both.

Kedgeree

SERVES 6–8

My friend Helen, who grew up in England with an Irish father and a mother from New Zealand, says that the taste of kedgeree will always bring her back, in an instant, to when she was little, sitting round the table with her family having brunch. It's a great recipe for feeding a crowd and, of course, it's good at any time of the day. This curried rice dish, made with delicious fresh or smoked fish, hard-boiled eggs and lots of intensely green parsley, is inspired by Helen's mum's recipe. Thanks, Beth!

450g (1lb) white or brown basmati rice
15g (½oz) butter
500g (1lb 2oz) smoked haddock (you could smoke your own as on page 152), skinned, deboned and cut into 2.5–5cm (1–2in) chunks
4 tbsp extra-virgin olive oil
2 large onions, thinly sliced
2 tsp ground cumin
2 tsp ground coriander
¼ tsp ground turmeric
pinch of cayenne pepper
½ tsp garam masala
8 eggs
225g (8oz) fresh or frozen peas
75ml (3fl oz) regular or double cream
2 tbsp chopped parsley
sea salt and freshly ground black pepper

1. Bring a large pan of water to the boil, add the rice with a good pinch of salt and cook over a medium heat, stirring from time to time, until tender – be careful not to overcook it or it will go mushy. White basmati rice will take only 10–12 minutes, while brown basmati rice will take 25–30 minutes to cook.

2. Place the butter in a frying pan over a medium-high heat and allow to melt and foam. Add the smoked fish pieces and 1 tablespoon water. Season with black pepper, turn the heat down slightly and cook, tossing regularly, until the fish is just opaque, 4–5 minutes.

3. Meanwhile, place a large frying pan over a high heat and heat the olive oil until hot, then add the sliced onions and sauté for 5 minutes, tossing regularly, until almost softened and golden at the edges. Add the ground cumin and coriander, the turmeric, cayenne pepper and garam masala. Turn the heat down to low, cover the pan with a lid and continue to cook the onions until they are completely softened, 5–8 minutes.

4. While the onions are cooking, bring a pot of water up to the boil, gently drop in the eggs and boil for just 6 or 7 minutes, depending on the size. When they are cooked, drain and pour cold water over them to stop them cooking. Once they are almost cool, peel the eggs, handling them gently as they'll be slightly soft in the centre.

5. Drop the peas into a pan of boiling water and boil for just 2 minutes or until cooked.

6. Once everything is cooked, you can assemble the dish. Add the drained rice and peas to the onions in the frying pan over a low heat and stir to mix.

Carefully stir in the fish with any lovely juices. Pour in the cream and half the chopped parsley and mix gently, then season with salt and pepper to taste.

7. Transfer to a wide, shallow serving bowl. Cut the eggs into quarters and arrange on top and around the sides, then sprinkle with the remaining chopped parsley and serve.

Devilled kidneys

A classic Victorian British breakfast dish, this would set you up for the day – and then some! Of course, it's great at any other time of the day, too, if kidneys are too hardcore for your morning ritual.

2 tbsp plain flour
¼ tsp cayenne pepper
¼ tsp grated nutmeg
1 tbsp sherry vinegar
1 tbsp Worcestershire sauce
1½ tsp Dijon mustard
90ml (3½fl oz) chicken stock
175ml (6fl oz) regular or double cream
25g (1oz) butter
6 lamb's kidneys, peeled, halved, all membranes removed, fat snipped from core, cut into 6 pieces (3 from each half)
sea salt and freshly ground black pepper

To serve
hot buttered toast or buttery mash

1. Mix the flour, cayenne pepper, nutmeg and a generous pinch of salt and pepper in a bowl and set aside.

2. In another bowl, combine the vinegar, Worcestershire sauce, Dijon mustard, chicken stock and cream, then set aside.

3. Heat the butter in a pan over a high heat. Toss the kidneys in the flour mix and, when the butter is foaming, cook the kidneys, turning them so that they brown on all sides. Next, pour in the cream mixture and allow it to bubble and thicken.

4. Serve on hot buttered toast or with buttery mashed potatoes.

Lunches

Chicken stock

MAKES 1.5–2 LITRES (2½–3½ PINTS) STOCK

I always have a pot of chicken stock on the go. When you're using good chickens for roasting or braising, it's crazy not to boil up the bones afterwards. There's an old South American proverb that says, 'Good broth will resurrect the dead,' and it's not far wrong as the nutritional content of a homemade stock indeed has miraculous qualities if eaten regularly. Our great-grandmothers were right after all.

1 whole chicken carcass, raw or cooked
1 large leek, cut into 4 pieces
2 celery sticks, each cut into 4 pieces
2 carrots, each cut into 4 pieces
2–4 garlic cloves, to taste, peeled
1 bouquet garni (a few sprigs of parsley, 1 or 2 sprigs of thyme and a small bay leaf)
a few black peppercorns
pinch of sea salt

1. Preheat the oven to 200°C (400°F), Gas mark 6. Place the chicken bones in a roasting tin and cook in the oven for 15 minutes. The roasting stage is optional but I love the slightly stronger, more enhanced flavour that it gives the final broth.

2. Once the bones are roasted (see tips), transfer them to a large saucepan and add the leek, celery, carrots and garlic cloves. Pop in the bouquet garni and black peppercorns, then cover generously with cold water – adding about 2 litres (3½ pints). The water must be cold since, while it's slowly heating up, it will draw the flavour and goodness out of the vegetables and the bones.

3. Bring to the boil, then turn the heat down and simmer for 2 hours, skimming off and discarding any foam that rises to the surface.

4. Once it's cooked, strain the broth through a fine sieve, then leave to stand to allow the fat to rise to the top. Skim off the fat and season the broth with salt to taste.

TIPS
If there are any bits of meat or little caramelised nuggets of flavour stuck to the roasting tin after cooking the chicken bones, place the tray over a medium heat on the hob, pour in a small glass of water and, using a whisk, scrape to dissolve the bits. Pour these into the saucepan too.

I've found that if I leave the fat sitting on top of the stock while it's in the fridge there are two added bonuses – once the fat is chilled it's far easier to lift it off the stock; and the stock keeps for longer (a few weeks rather than just a few days) in the fridge if completely covered in the fat. Remove the fat before use.

Chicken noodle broth

SERVES 6–8

I remember many versions of this broth while growing up – I don't think it was ever the same twice. Mum seemed to constantly have a delicious chicken stock on the go, which always went into this most restorative of soups – a hug in a bowl.

1.6 litres (2¾ pints) chicken stock, well strained
4 garlic cloves, finely sliced
160g (5½oz) spaghetti, broken into 2.5cm (1in) lengths
4 tbsp chopped parsley
sea salt and freshly ground black pepper

1. Put the chicken stock, garlic and spaghetti into a saucepan and season with a pinch of salt and pepper. Cover and bring to a gentle boil, then turn the heat down and simmer for 8–10 minutes until the spaghetti is cooked (or cook for the length of time specified on the packet).

2. When the spaghetti is cooked, stir in the parsley, check the seasoning and serve.

Chicken broth with chilli and ginger

SERVES 4

1.2 litres (2 pints) cold chicken or vegetable stock, well strained
20 large sprigs of coriander or flat-leaf parsley, stalks and leaves separated
½–1 red chilli, to taste, finely sliced (leave the seeds in if you dare!)
2cm (¾ inch) piece of fresh ginger, finely sliced
sea salt and freshly ground black pepper

1. Put the cold stock in a saucepan and add the coriander or parsley stalks (keep the leaves for serving), sliced chilli, ginger and a little salt and pepper. Bring to the boil, then taste and add more seasoning, if you like.

2. Ladle into warm bowls or cups and serve scattered with the coriander or parsley leaves – whole or chopped, whichever you prefer.

My mum, Hallfridur, with her mum, Ragga, or Amma as I call her.

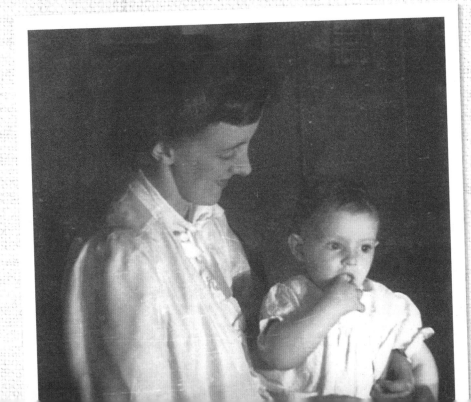

Chicken dumpling soup

SERVES 4

A twist on the age-old Asian dumpling soup, this is deeply satisfying and wonderfully restorative. The better the chicken stock, the better the soup.

300g (11oz) minced chicken (thigh is best but breast works fine too)
1 small garlic clove, crushed
2 tbsp chopped parsley
¼ tsp grated nutmeg
60g (2½oz) spring onions, white parts finely chopped and green parts sliced at an angle, kept separate
a little oil
1.5 litres (2½ pints) chicken stock
handful of broken spaghetti (optional)
sea salt and freshly ground black pepper

1. Place the minced chicken in a bowl and add the garlic, parsley, ¼ teaspoon salt, the nutmeg and a twist of black pepper. Add the white parts of the spring onions and mix well to combine. Break off a small piece of the mixture and fry it in a little oil, then taste it and adjust the seasoning if needed.

2. With wet hands, shape the minced chicken into 20 equal-sized dumplings. Set aside in the fridge while you prepare your chicken broth.

3. Pour the stock into a saucepan, add salt and pepper if necessary, and bring it to the boil. Add the chicken dumplings and bring to a gentle simmer for 10 minutes to cook the dumplings through. (If you want to make this soup more substantial, add a handful of broken spaghetti strands and cook with the stock and the dumplings.)

4. Add the green parts of the spring onions for the last minute of cooking. Divide the broth and the dumplings among four bowls and serve.

Chorizo, bean and kale broth

SERVES 6

I have a problem with chorizo, in that I cannot get enough of the stuff. It has an amazing ability to give its characteristic kick to everything – from chicken and shellfish to pulses and grains. This is the kind of chunky soup that I adore; full of flavour and bursting with goodness.

125g (4½oz) dried borlotti beans, haricot or butter beans (or use 250g/9oz tinned beans, drained and rinsed)
1 tbsp extra-virgin olive oil
1 red onion, chopped
1 carrot, chopped
1 celery stick, chopped
1 garlic clove, chopped
110g (4oz) chorizo, skin removed, cut into dice
200g (7oz) tomatoes, chopped
1.2 litres (2 pints) chicken or vegetable stock
75g (3oz) de-stalked kale, roughly chopped
1 tbsp chopped parsley
1 tbsp chopped rosemary
pinch of grated nutmeg
sea salt and freshly ground black pepper

To serve
crusty bread

1. First prepare the beans, if using dried beans. Soak the dried beans in plenty of cold water overnight. The next day, drain and place in a pan of fresh cold water and boil for 45–60 minutes until tender. Drain and set aside.

2. Heat the olive oil in a saucepan over a medium-low heat. Add the onion, carrot, celery and garlic with a pinch of salt and pepper. Sweat for 15 minutes with the lid on until the onion is soft but not coloured.

3. Add the diced chorizo, replace the lid and continue to cook for a further 5 minutes to let the oils run out.

4. Next, add the freshly cooked or drained tinned beans and tomatoes, cover and cook for a further 5 minutes. Then, add the stock, bring to the boil, then simmer for 5 minutes more.

5. Finally, add the kale, parsley, rosemary and nutmeg, and cook, uncovered, for 5–10 minutes until the kale is tender. The cooking time will depend on the time of year, as young kale cooks quicker. Serve with crusty bread.

Oxtail and pearl barley soup

SERVES 4–6

A deeply satisfying meal in a bowl, this is the very essence of comfort food.
Hearty, nutritious and frugal to boot, what's not to love?

90g (3¼oz) pearl barley
25g (1oz) butter
1 oxtail, about 1kg (2lb
    3oz), cut into pieces
    4–6cm (1½–2in) long, cut
    through the 'knuckles'
3 carrots, cut into large
    chunks
1 leek, cut into large chunks
2 celery sticks, cut into large
    chunks
1 large or 2 small onions,
    cut into large chunks
3 garlic cloves, halved
100ml (3½fl oz) red
    wine
4 tbsp sherry vinegar
1 bouquet garni (a few
    sprigs of parsley, 1 or 2
    sprigs of thyme and a
    small bay leaf)
2 tbsp tomato purée
good pinch of salt
15 peppercorns
4 tbsp chopped parsley
juice of ¼ lemon

1. Preheat the oven to 150°C (300°F), Gas mark 2. Put the pearl barley into a heatproof bowl and pour in 270ml (9½fl oz) boiling water to cover. Set aside.

2. Melt the butter in a large casserole over a medium heat. Add the chunks of oxtail and brown on all sides, then transfer to a bowl or plate. Brown the vegetables and garlic, then pour in the wine and vinegar and scrape up the dark caramelised bits with a wooden spoon. Return the oxtail to the casserole. Next, pour in 1.5 litres (2½ pints) water and add the bouquet garni, tomato purée, salt and peppercorns. Bring to the boil, then transfer to the oven, or simmer very gently on the hob, for 3–3½ hours until the meat is falling off the bone. Carefully remove the pieces of oxtail from the casserole and put on a tray to cool slightly.

3. Meanwhile, strain the vegetables and discard, then strain the cooking liquor into another heatproof bowl. Clean the casserole and pour in the strained liquid. Allow to stand until the fat rises to the top, then skim it off. Strain the pearl barley and add it to the skimmed liquid.

4. It's a bit fiddly, but pick all the meat from the cooled oxtail bones and discard the bones and fat. This takes a little while but it is worth it. Pull the meat apart with your fingers then add the shreds to the casserole with the skimmed liquid and pearl barley and cook for 45 minutes over a medium heat. Taste and adjust the seasoning.

5. Stir in the parsley and lemon juice, then serve immediately.

Salmon, smoked haddock and pea chowder

SERVES 4–6

A chowder is a great way to make a little fish go a long way, and smoked haddock brings its own lovely richness. This is delicious served with Sue's Oatmeal Bread on page 204.

50g (2oz) butter
120g (4oz) leeks, halved lengthways, then cut into 5mm (¼in) slices
150g (5oz) spring onions, green and white parts sliced, kept separate
600g (1lb 5oz) potatoes, cut into 1cm (½in) dice
1 litre (1¾ pints) light chicken, fish or vegetable stock
120g (4oz) smoked haddock fillet, cut into 1–2cm (½–¾in) chunks
200g (7oz) salmon fillet, cut into 1–2cm (½–¾in) chunks
100g (3½oz) peas
50ml (2fl oz) regular or double cream
3 tbsp chopped parsley

1. Melt the butter in a large pan and add the leeks, the white parts of the spring onions and the potatoes. Cook over a low heat for 10 minutes or until the leeks and spring onions are soft but not coloured.

2. Add the stock and bring it to the boil, then turn down and simmer for 15 minutes or until the potatoes are soft.

3. Add the smoked haddock, salmon, peas and the green parts of the spring onions. Cook for a further 5 minutes, then add the cream and chopped parsley and cook for a further 2–3 minutes. Serve piping hot.

Crab and sweetcorn chowder

SERVES 4–6

A chowder is more than just a soup, it's a meal in a bowl, and this version with delicious sweet-salty crabmeat and corn is a keeper. Needless to say, the better the crabmeat, the more delicious this will be. If you can get hold of some brown crabmeat along with the white, the flavour will be even better.

30g (1¼oz) butter
200g (7oz) onions, cut into 1cm (½in) dice
2 garlic cloves, chopped
300g (11oz) potatoes, cut into 1cm (½in) dice
600ml (1 pint) hot chicken, fish or vegetable stock
200g (7oz) sweetcorn kernels
200ml (7fl oz) milk
150g (5oz) white crabmeat
pinch of cayenne pepper
1 tbsp lemon juice
2 tbsp chopped parsley
2 tsp chopped tarragon
50ml (2fl oz) regular or double cream
sea salt and freshly ground black pepper

To serve
fresh bread

1. Melt the butter in a saucepan over a gentle heat, then add the onions and garlic with a little salt and pepper. Cover and allow to sweat until soft but not coloured. Add the potatoes and cook for a further 5–10 minutes, stirring occasionally so that they don't brown.

2. Next, add the stock, sweetcorn and milk, and bring to the boil, then lower the heat and simmer until the potatoes are cooked through and are just beginning to thicken the soup.

3. Finally, add the crabmeat, cayenne pepper, lemon juice, chopped herbs and cream. Bring the chowder back up to a gentle simmer, then serve with lots of lovely bread.

Wild garlic soup

A vibrant green soup that makes you feel good just looking at it, not to mention eating it! Use the wide-leaf wild garlic, ramson, or the three-cornered leek with the narrow leaves, both in season in spring. At other times of the year, or if you can't get hold of any wild garlic, you can replace it with watercress, young nettles (wear gloves when harvesting – the sting will go once cooked!), spinach, kale or chard.

25g (1oz) butter
2 potatoes, diced
1 onion, chopped
1 litre (1¾ pints) chicken or
   vegetable stock
2 large handfuls of wild
   garlic leaves, roughly
   chopped
110ml (4fl oz) regular or
   double cream
sea salt and freshly ground
   black pepper

To serve
crusty bread

1. Melt the butter in a large saucepan over a medium heat. When foaming, add the potatoes and onion, and toss in the butter until well coated, then season with salt and pepper. Turn the heat down, cover the pan and cook for 10 minutes or until the vegetables are soft, stirring regularly so that the vegetables don't stick and burn.

2. Next, add the stock and bring to a rolling boil, then add the wild garlic leaves and cook for 2 minutes or until the leaves have wilted. Don't overcook the soup at this stage or it will lose its fresh green colour and flavour.

3. Immediately pour into a blender and whiz until smooth, then return to the clean pan, stir in the cream and taste for seasoning.

4. Serve hot with crusty bread.

Beetroot soup with chives

SERVES 8–10

I remember my mum started making beetroot soup for dinner parties in the 1980s and back then I thought the vivid pink concoction was the epitome of chic. I still do, and love it that something so stunningly pretty can be that good for you.

900g (2lb) whole raw
  beetroot
25g (1oz) butter
225g (8oz) onions, chopped
1.2 litres (2 pints) chicken or
  vegetable stock
110ml (4fl oz) cream or
  milk, or a mixture
sea salt and freshly ground
  black pepper

To serve
110g (4oz) sour cream or
  crème fraîche
2 tbsp finely chopped chives

1. Remove the leaves from the beetroot (use these for another recipe), then cut off most of the stalk, leaving about 2cm (¾in) still attached to the root. Leave the tails of the beetroot intact. Wash the beetroot carefully under a cold tap. Do not scrub them – simply rub off any dirt with your fingers. You don't want to damage the skin or to cut off the top or tails, otherwise the beetroot will 'bleed' while cooking, losing important nutrients.

2. Place the beetroot in a saucepan and cover with cold water and a pinch of salt. Place over a medium heat and bring to a simmer. Cover, then continue to simmer for 30 minutes–2 hours, depending on the size and age of your beetroot. They are cooked when their skins rub off easily and a knife just slides into the centre.

3. While the beetroot cooks, melt the butter in a large saucepan over a low heat. When melted, add the onions and season with salt and pepper. Cover and cook for 8–10 minutes until soft but not coloured.

4. When the beetroot is cooked, rub off the skins and discard, then cut into chunks. Add to the onions with the stock. Bring to a rolling boil, then pour into a blender and whiz until it is quite smooth (be careful, beetroot will stain). Return to the pan over a medium heat, stir in the cream and/or milk, then taste and adjust the seasoning.

5. Serve hot, topped with a spoonful of sour cream or crème fraîche and a scattering of chives.

Almost-instant tomato and basil soup

SERVES 4

A delicious fresh-tasting soup that's super-quick to make, this is like summer in a bowl. Like many soups, it can be frozen, too, for a taste of summer in any season!

25g (1oz) butter
125g (4½oz) white parts of spring onions, chopped (keep the green tops for another recipe)
1 garlic clove, chopped
400g (14oz) very ripe tomatoes, chopped or 1 x 400g tin chopped tomatoes
generous pinch of sugar
400ml (14fl oz) hot vegetable or chicken stock
50ml (2fl oz) regular or double cream
sea salt and freshly ground black pepper

To serve
1 tbsp chopped basil or 4 tsp basil pesto

1. Melt the butter in a saucepan over a medium heat, then add the spring onions and garlic and season with salt and pepper. Cover the pan and sweat the onions for 5 minutes. Add the tomatoes and sugar. Turn up the heat and bring to the boil, then turn the heat down and simmer for 5 minutes. Add the stock, bring to the boil, then turn down the heat and simmer for a further 5 minutes. Add the cream and simmer for just 1 minute.

2. Transfer to a blender and whiz really well. Pour the soup through a fine sieve into a clean pan and gently reheat but do not boil the soup.

3. To serve, stir in the chopped basil or drizzle the basil pesto over each bowl.

Warm salad of hot-smoked duck, glazed navettes and toasted hazelnuts

SERVES 4

Duck reacts so well to a bit of hot smoke – the rich flavour of the meat is enhanced by its full-bodied aroma and the lovely layer of fat under the skin ensures the meat does not dry out during smoking. The little white turnips, called navettes, end up tender and coated in a delicious glaze set against the welcome crunch of the hazelnuts.

32 hazelnuts, chopped into 2 or 3 pieces and toasted (see tip)
4 navettes (small white turnips), cut into 6 or 8 wedges
15g (½oz) butter
2 duck breasts
4 good handfuls of bitter greens (watercress, rocket, mustard leaf, frisée)
sea salt and freshly ground black pepper

For the dressing
1 tbsp good-quality sherry vinegar
3 tbsp hazelnut or walnut oil
1 tsp Dijon mustard

1. Place all the dressing ingredients in a bowl, season with salt and pepper and whisk well to combine. Set aside.

2. Place the navettes in a flameproof casserole or small saucepan. Add 3 tablespoons water and the butter, and season with salt and pepper. Cover with a tight-fitting lid and cook for 20 minutes over a medium heat. Check the navettes while they are cooking and remove the lid for the last few minutes of cooking time if there is still a lot of liquid in the casserole. They should be glazed but not wet.

3. Meanwhile, following the instructions for the Biscuit-Tin-Smoked Fish on page 152, put your duck breasts into the biscuit-tin smoker to smoke for 20 minutes while the navettes are cooking.

4. When the duck is smoked and the navettes are cooked, slice the duck breasts. Arrange the sliced duck and navette wedges in a circle around the edge of four warm plates, leaving a space in the middle of each plate for the salad.

5. Dress the bitter greens with most of the dressing and divide among the plates. Sprinkle with the toasted hazelnuts and drizzle with the remaining dressing. Serve immediately.

TIP
Tip the hazelnuts into a non-stick frying pan and toast over a high heat for 1–2 minutes until golden, tossing regularly to avoid burning. Take off the heat and set aside to cool.

Salad of smoked fish with lamb's lettuce and a crispy egg

SERVES 4

A gorgeously substantial salad, this has all the elements of a summer main course that I love – delicious fresh leaves, smoky tender fish and a softly boiled egg encased in a crispy breadcrumb coating. Use really good extra-virgin olive oil here.

4 x 200g (7oz) fillets of fish
– smoked haddock or
coley, either hot-smoked
(see Biscuit-Tin-Smoked
Fish, see page 152),
or shop-bought cold-
smoked fish
a little butter
4 handfuls of lamb's lettuce
or any other delicious
salad leaves

For the dressing
2 tsp Dijon mustard
2 tsp white wine vinegar
2 tbsp extra-virgin olive oil
sea salt and freshly ground
black pepper

For the crispy eggs
4 eggs, plus 1 beaten egg
2 tbsp plain flour, seasoned
with salt and pepper
3 tbsp panko or fine white
breadcrumbs
sunflower oil, for shallow-
frying or deep-frying

1. To make the crispy eggs, bring a large pan of water to the boil, then add the eggs (they need to be completely submerged), set a timer and allow to boil for exactly 5 minutes. Using a slotted spoon, remove the eggs and cool under cold running water to prevent them cooking further.

2. Place the seasoned flour, beaten egg and the breadcrumbs in three separate shallow dishes. Peel the eggs carefully, as they will still be soft in the centre, roll them in the flour, then in the beaten egg and, finally, in the crumbs to give them a nice coating. Set aside.

3. Cook your fish – either follow the hot-smoked biscuit-tin recipe on page 152, or pan-fry the cold-smoked fish in a little butter.

4. While the fish is cooking, heat a little sunflower oil for the crispy eggs in a small pan and shallow-fry the eggs, turning frequently, until they are golden and crispy all over, or deep-fry them in sunflower oil.

5. Whisk together all the ingredients for the dressing. Put the lamb's lettuce in a bowl and sprinkle with a few teaspoons of the dressing, then toss – the leaves should be lightly coated but not too much.

6. Place the cooked fish in the centre of each plate, then place a crispy egg on top. Arrange the dressed leaves around each one in a ring, drizzle the whole plate with more dressing and serve.

Roast beetroot salad with liquorice, goat's cheese and candied pearl barley

SERVES 4

This salad is inspired by a recipe that the wonderful cookery writer Diana Henry wrote on her return from my mother's home town of Reykjavik. Liquorice is one of my mum's favourite flavours from growing up in Iceland and this is an intriguing method of cooking it with beetroot. It adds a subtle, spicy sweetness, but you can leave it out if you prefer.

400g (14oz) even-sized raw beetroot, whole and unpeeled
2 sticks (20g/¾oz) broken liquorice root
4 handfuls of salad leaves, including some small beetroot leaves, if possible
150g (5oz) soft goat's cheese

For the candied pearl barley
50g (2oz) pearl barley
50g (2oz) brown sugar
pinch of sea salt

For the dressing
4 tbsp extra-virgin olive oil
4 tbsp walnut oil
1 tbsp honey
2 tbsp cider vinegar
1 tbsp Dijon mustard
sea salt and freshly ground black pepper

1. Remove the leaves from the beetroot and cut off most of the stalk, leaving about 2cm (¾in) attached. Leave the tails intact. Wash under a cold tap – do not scrub, simply rub off any dirt with your fingers. You don't want to damage the skin, otherwise the beetroot will 'bleed' while cooking, losing important nutrients.

2. Put the beets in a saucepan large enough to fit them all in a tight single layer, add the liquorice and just cover with water – do not add salt. Cover, place on the hob and bring to the boil, then turn the heat down and simmer for ¾–1 hour until cooked. The skin should peel easily and a knife slide into the centre.

3. Using a slotted spoon, remove the beetroot and set aside until cool enough to handle. Return the pot to the hob and allow the beetroot cooking water to bubble with the lid off until reduced to a quarter of its original volume. Discard the liquorice.

4. While the beets cook, toast the pearl barley in a pan over a medium heat, shaking frequently until it turns a light nutty brown. Remove from the pan and set aside.

5. Sprinkle the brown sugar into the dry pan, return to the heat and, without stirring, allow to dissolve. When the sugar has dissolved, return the pearl barley to the pan with a pinch of salt. Shake the pan or swirl gently to coat the pearl barley with caramel and then pour it out onto a piece of baking parchment. Set aside to cool.

6. Next, make the dressing. Mix the oils, honey, vinegar and mustard in a bowl with a pinch of salt. Set aside.

7. Preheat the oven to 200°C (400°F), Gas mark 6. When cool, peel the beets and cut into wedges. Toss in a little dressing and roast for 10 minutes.

8. Loosen the remaining dressing with 1 tablespoon of the beetroot cooking liquid. Dress the leaves, divide among four plates in a 'nest' in the centre of each. Alternate wedges of beetroot and blobs of cheese around the leaves. Chop the candied pearl barley and sprinkle over, drizzle with the remaining dressing and serve.

Scandi kale salad with horseradish

A lovely simple salad with Scandi flavours that uses lots of nutritious raw kale.
The deliciously hot/sweet/tangy dressing is also super tossed with raw grated
beetroot, carrot and celeriac, slaw-style.

200g (7oz) de-stalked kale
   leaves, roughly chopped

For the dressing
175g (6oz) crème fraîche
120ml (4fl oz) lemon juice
2½ tbsp finely grated
   horseradish
40g (1½oz) sugar
pinch of sea salt

1. Place the kale leaves in a bowl.

2. To make the dressing, whisk together the crème fraîche, lemon juice,
   horseradish and sugar, and season with a pinch of salt. Add the dressing to
   the kale and toss to combine.

Beetroot and coriander hummus

1 raw beetroot, peeled and
   cut into chunks
1 x 400g tin of chickpeas,
   drained and rinsed
2 garlic cloves, crushed
2 tbsp light tahini (sesame
   seed paste)
3 tbsp extra-virgin olive oil,
   plus extra if needed
juice of ½–1 lemon, to taste
2 tbsp chopped coriander
sea salt and freshly ground
   black pepper

1. Place the beetroot chunks, chickpeas, garlic and tahini into a food processor,
   pour in the olive oil, then pulse until smooth. Add the lemon juice and the
   chopped coriander then season to taste with salt and pepper. If the hummus
   is a bit too thick, add a little more olive oil.

2. The hummus will keep in the fridge in a sealed container for three to
   four days. Use as a dip for raw vegetable sticks or pitta bread, or as a salad
   dressing.

Chicken burger with lemon and chive mayonnaise

MAKES 6–8 BURGERS

This is comfort food in a bun. It's up to you whether you use brown or white meat for mincing, but I find that a mixture of the two works well to give a deliciously flavoursome and juicy burger. The lemon and chive mayonnaise is the perfect accompaniment.

25g (1oz) butter
300g (11oz) shallots, finely
    sliced, or 1 red onion,
    finely chopped
4 garlic cloves, crushed
2 tbsp chopped thyme
900g (2lb) minced chicken
zest of 1 lemon
1–2 tbsp extra-virgin
    olive oil
salt and freshly ground
    black pepper

For the lemon and chive
    mayonnaise
2 tbsp snipped chives
2 tbsp of lemon juice, plus
    extra to taste
1 tsp Dijon mustard
generous pinch of salt
2 egg yolks
50ml (2fl oz) extra-virgin
    olive oil
150ml (5fl oz) sunflower oil

To serve
Buttermilk Burger Buns
    (page 207)
fresh rocket
slices of ripe tomatoes

1. First make the mayonnaise. Put all the ingredients, except the oils, in a glass bowl (a stainless-steel bowl can give the mayonnaise a grey colour). Mix the oils in a jug. Continuously whisk the mixture in the bowl while adding the oil slowly in a thin, steady stream until it is completely combined to a smooth, creamy texture. Taste for seasoning and add an extra splash of lemon juice if necessary. (For speed, you can use an electric hand whisk.) Cover and chill while you make the burgers.

2. Melt the butter in a saucepan, then add the shallots or onion, the garlic, thyme, and salt and pepper to taste. Put the lid on the pan and sweat over a gentle heat until the onions are soft but not coloured. Remove from the heat and allow to cool.

3. Combine the minced chicken, cooled onion mixture and the lemon zest in a bowl and season with salt and pepper. Break off a small piece and fry it in a little oil, then taste it and adjust the seasoning if needed.

4. Use your hands to shape the mixture into 6 large or 8 medium burgers, each with a thickness of roughly 2cm (¾ in) – having wet hands makes this much easier to do.

5. Preheat a griddle or frying pan over a high heat, then turn the heat down to medium and add the olive oil. Fry the burgers for 8–10 minutes on each side to cook through, turning the heat down to low once the burgers are golden on both sides. You may need to do this in two batches, adding more olive oil when frying the second batch. (You can finish them in the oven preheated to 200°C (400°F), Gas mark 6 for 5–8 minutes until cooked through, if you want to.)

6. Serve in a bun with some rocket, tomato slices and a good blob of the lemon and chive mayonnaise.

Pork burgers

The fresh, summery mayonnaise works a treat with this great pork burger.

900g (2lb) minced pork
150g (5oz) spring onions,
    finely chopped
2 garlic cloves, crushed
1–2 tbsp extra-virgin olive
    oil
6–8 slices of mozzarella
    cheese
sea salt and freshly ground
    black pepper

For the tomato and basil
    mayonnaise
2 tsp tomato purée
1 tsp Dijon mustard
1 tbsp chopped basil
1 tbsp red wine vinegar
pinch of sea salt
2 egg yolks
50ml (2fl oz) extra-virgin
    olive oil
150ml (5fl oz) sunflower oil

To serve
Buttermilk Burger Buns
    (page 207)
cucumber slices

1. First make the mayonnaise. Put all the ingredients, except the oils, in a glass bowl (a stainless-steel bowl can give the mayonnaise a grey colour). Mix the oils in a jug. Continuously whisk the mixture in the bowl while adding the oil slowly in a thin, steady stream until it is completely combined to a smooth, creamy texture. Taste for seasoning. (For speed, you can use an electric hand whisk.) Cover and chill while you make the burgers.

2. Next make the burgers. Mix the pork, spring onions, garlic, and salt and pepper in a bowl. Break off a small piece and fry it in a little oil, then taste it and adjust the seasoning if needed.

3. Use your hands to shape the mixture into 6 large or 8 medium-sized burgers, 1–2cm (½–¾in) thick.

4. Place a frying pan over a medium heat and heat the olive oil. Fry the burgers for 8–10 minutes on each side over a medium-low heat. You may need to do this in two batches, adding more olive oil when frying the second batch. When the burgers are nearly cooked, place a slice of mozzarella cheese on each burger, cover the pan with a lid and cook until the cheese has melted.

5. Serve in a fresh bun with some sliced cucumber and a blob of tomato and basil mayonnaise.

Beetroot and hazelnut slaw

A slaw is just the thing to serve with rich meats at a barbecue, or indeed burgers. It's both a salad and a sauce that'll bring freshness and crunch.

225g (8oz) raw beetroot, peeled and grated
225g (8oz) carrot, grated
3 tbsp chopped mint or parsley
¼ head of savoy cabbage
4 tbsp hazelnut oil or extra-virgin olive oil
2 tbsp lemon juice
2 tsp Dijon mustard
110g (4oz) hazelnuts, toasted and roughly chopped (see tip, page 58)
sea salt and freshly ground black pepper

1. Place the grated beetroot and carrot and the chopped mint or parsley in a large bowl. Remove the dark outer leaves from the cabbage, cut out and discard the core and shred the leaves as thinly as possible, cutting across the quartered head. Add the cabbage to the bowl.

2. In a small bowl, combine the oil and lemon juice with the Dijon mustard, then season with salt and pepper. Pour the dressing onto the vegetables and herbs and mix well until evenly coated.

3. Transfer to a serving bowl or plate, scatter over the toasted hazelnuts and serve.

Beef burgers

MAKES 6–8 BURGERS

Every committed carnivore needs a decent burger recipe in their repertoire, and this simple beef burger should tick the box for you. The horseradish and tarragon mayonnaise is super with a steak or lamb chops, too.

25g (1oz) butter
300g (11oz) onions, finely chopped
900g (2lb) minced beef
2 tbsp chopped thyme, marjoram and parsley (preferably a mixture)
1 egg, beaten
1–2 tbsp extra-virgin olive oil
sea salt and freshly ground black pepper

1. First make the mayonnaise. Put all the ingredients, except the oils, in a glass bowl (a stainless-steel bowl can give the mayonnaise a grey colour). Mix the oils in a jug. Continuously whisk the mixture in the bowl while adding the oil slowly in a thin, steady stream until it is completely combined to a smooth, creamy texture. Taste for seasoning. (For speed, you can use an electric hand whisk.) Cover and chill while you make the burgers.

2. Melt the butter in a saucepan over a medium-low heat, then add the onions and cook for 6–8 minutes until they are completely soft and a pale gold colour. Take off the heat and allow to cool completely.

3. Meanwhile, mix the mince with the herbs and egg and season with salt and pepper. Add the cooled onions and mix together thoroughly. Break off a small piece of the mixture and fry it in a little oil, then taste it and adjust the seasoning if needed.

For the horseradish and
tarragon mayonnaise
2 tsp finely grated fresh
    horseradish
2 tsp Dijon mustard
2 tsp chopped tarragon
1 tbsp cider vinegar
pinch of salt
2 egg yolks
50ml (2fl oz) extra-virgin
    olive oil
150ml (5fl oz) sunflower oil

To serve
Buttermilk Burger Buns
    (page 207)
sliced lettuce and gherkins

4. Next, use your hands to shape the mixture into 6 large or 8 medium-sized burgers, 1–2cm (½–¾in) thick.

5. Place a frying pan over a medium heat and heat the olive oil. Fry the burgers for 4–7 minutes on each side depending on the thickness and how well done you like your burger. You may need to do this in two batches, adding more olive oil when frying the second batch.

6. Serve on burger buns with lettuce and gherkins and a blob of horseradish and tarragon mayonnaise.

My mum, Hallfridur, with her little sister, Kristin, in the bonnet.

Creamy pork and tomato pasta

SERVES 4–6

My mum used to make lots of great comforting pasta dishes like this when we were little, but no two ever seemed to be the same. In fact, when I asked her for one of her recipes, she just said that she used to make it up as she went along! So here is my version of one of Mum's delicious concoctions – I hope you like it as much as I do.

500g (1lb 2oz) pasta, such as pappardelle or tagliatelle
25g (1oz) butter
250g (9oz) onions, chopped
4 garlic cloves, finely sliced
400g (14oz) minced pork
1 tbsp chopped sage
a little grated nutmeg
2 tbsp extra-virgin olive oil
400g (14oz) tomatoes, peeled and chopped (see tip, page 114), or 1 x 400g tin of chopped tomatoes
pinch of sugar
2 tbsp chopped parsley
150ml (5fl oz) regular or double cream
sea salt and freshly ground black pepper

1. Bring a large saucepan of water to the boil with 1 teaspoon salt, add the pasta and cook for the length of time specified in the packet instructions or until al dente.

2. While the pasta is cooking, melt the butter in a saucepan. Add the onions and garlic, cover the pan with a lid and sweat the vegetables until soft but not coloured. Season with salt and pepper.

3. While the onions and garlic are sweating, mix the pork with the chopped sage, then season with grated nutmeg, salt and pepper.

4. When the onions and garlic are soft, remove them from the pan and set aside.

5. Add the olive oil to the pan and return to a medium heat. When the oil is hot, add the pork in little pieces pinched off with your fingers, or with a teaspoon. Fry the pork on all sides until golden, then return the onions and garlic to the pan and add the tomatoes, season again with a pinch of salt and pepper and a pinch of sugar. When the tomatoes have cooked down to half their original volume, add the parsley and cream and cook for a further 2–3 minutes to thicken slightly.

6. Drain the pasta, strain the pasta but reserve about 100ml (3½fl oz) of the cooking water – this is very useful for adding into the pasta sauce if it's too thick, or stirring into the pasta itself if you're waiting for the sauce to cook and the pasta starts sticking. Add the sauce to the pasta, mix well to combine, adding a little pasta cooking water if it needs loosening, then serve immediately.

Lamb's liver on toast with whiskey, garlic, thyme and cream

SERVES 4 AS A STARTER

A quick supper dish that makes the most of the great pairing that is liver and whiskey.

300g (11oz) lamb's liver, cut into 2.5cm (1in) chunks
200ml (7fl oz) milk
4 slices of bread
25g (1oz) butter, plus extra for the toast
1 garlic clove, finely chopped
2 tsp thyme leaves, roughly chopped
60ml (2½fl oz) whiskey
100ml (3½fl oz) regular or double cream

1. Soak the lamb's liver in the milk in a deep bowl for 30 minutes.

2. Toast the bread, butter the slices, then place them on plates and keep warm in the oven.

3. Melt the butter in a large pan over a high heat. Pat the liver dry on kitchen paper. When the butter is foaming, add the liver and fry until deep golden and crisp. Add the garlic and thyme and fry for just 1 minute more until the garlic is light golden.

4. Next, add the whiskey. If you are using gas, tilt the pan carefully towards the flame, otherwise hold a match near the edge of the pan. Either method should cause the alcohol to flare up, so be careful not to burn yourself. When the flame dies down, add the cream and allow it to bubble until the contents of the pan reduce to a quite thick creamy sauce.

5. Spoon the liver and sauce over the buttered toast and enjoy!

Liver, bacon and onions

SERVES 4

This recipe is inspired by hearing my friend Patricia talk about her mum's cooking as she was growing up. As in many Irish and British houses, offal made a regular appearance in home cooking. Patricia's mum, Maura O'Brien, cooked liver once a week and always, says Patricia, on the day that it came from the butcher, so it was nice and fresh.

600g (1lb 5oz) lamb's liver, cut into 8 slices, 1.5cm (⅝in) thick
300ml (½ pint) milk
50g (2oz) butter
150g (5oz) onions, sliced
100g (3½oz) streaky bacon, cut into 1cm (½in) strips (lardons)
2 garlic cloves, sliced very thinly
25g (1oz) plain flour
2 tbsp chopped parsley
sea salt and freshly ground black pepper

To serve
buttered toast (optional)

1. Soak the liver in the milk for at least 30 minutes.

2. Heat half the butter in a frying pan, add the onions, bacon and garlic and season with salt and pepper. Fry gently, so that the garlic doesn't burn, until the bacon becomes crispy and the onions and garlic are golden. Remove from the pan and set aside.

3. Mix the flour with a generous pinch of salt and pepper. Pat the liver dry on kitchen paper, then toss in the seasoned flour to coat.

4. Melt the remaining butter in the frying pan, then add the slices of liver and fry on both sides to a nice crispy finish. Return the onions, bacon and garlic to the frying pan and heat through with the liver.

5. Divide among four warm plates, sprinkle each plate with a little chopped parsley and serve with lots of buttery toast, if you like.

Pasta with smoked salmon, bacon and cream

SERVES 4–6

A supper that features regularly at our house, this pasta dish makes a little smoked salmon go a long way. The salty, rich, smoked fish loves a fresh green vegetable as a companion: peas, broad beans, broccoli and asparagus all work a treat.

500g (1lb 2oz) pasta, such as pappardelle or tagliatelle
a knob of butter
100g (3½oz) streaky bacon, cut into 1cm (½in) strips (lardons)
100g (3½oz) frozen peas
150g (5oz) smoked salmon, cut into 1cm (½in) cubes
150ml (5fl oz) regular or double cream
good squeeze of lemon juice
1 tbsp chopped parsley or a mixture of parsley, chives and dill
sea salt and freshly ground black pepper

1. Bring a large saucepan of water to the boil with 1 teaspoon salt, add the pasta and cook for the length of time specified in the packet instructions or until al dente.

2. When cooked, strain the pasta but reserve about 100ml (3½fl oz) of the cooking water – this is very useful for adding into the pasta sauce if it's too thick, or stirring into the pasta itself if you're waiting for the sauce to cook and the pasta starts sticking. You don't need to add oil or butter to the pasta once it's drained.

3. While the pasta is cooking, place a saucepan or frying pan over a medium heat and add the knob of butter. When melted, tip in the lardons and cook for a few minutes until the fat has rendered out and the bacon is golden. Add the peas and smoked salmon and stir over the heat for a minute or two until the salmon begins to cook, then pour in the cream and boil, uncovered, for 2 minutes until slightly thickened. Add the lemon juice, chopped herbs and some salt and pepper to taste.

4. Tip the pasta into the sauce and mix, adding a little pasta cooking water if it needs loosening. Taste again for seasoning and serve.

Linguine with crab, garlic, chilli and parsley

SERVES 4–6

One of my favourite pasta dishes of all, this classic pairing of sweet crabmeat with savoury garlic, chilli and parsley also happens to be the fastest supper around. Don't forget to hang on to some of the pasta cooking water to add back in if it starts to dry out.

500g (1lb 2oz) linguine, or other pasta, if you prefer
45g (1¾oz) butter
3 tbsp extra-virgin olive oil
2 garlic cloves, sliced
¼–½ red chilli, to taste, deseeded and chopped
250g (9oz) white and some brown crabmeat (if possible)
4 tbsp chopped parsley
sea salt and freshly ground black pepper

To serve
grated Parmesan cheese

1. Bring a large saucepan of water to the boil, add the pasta and stir in 1 teaspoon salt, then cook for the length of time specified in the packet instructions or until al dente.

2. While the pasta is cooking, melt the butter with the olive oil in a pot over a medium heat. Add the garlic, chilli, salt and pepper. Cook until the garlic is just beginning to turn a pale golden colour, then remove from the heat and set aside.

3. When the pasta is cooked, drain it, reserving about 100ml (3½fl oz) of the cooking water. Pour the garlic-chilli butter into the pasta cooking pot, add the crabmeat and return to the heat to warm the crab through. Add the drained pasta and toss with the sauce to coat – add a little of the retained cooking water if it looks too dry. Finally, stir in the chopped parsley and serve with grated Parmesan.

Smoked haddock, potato and chorizo tortilla omelette

SERVES 4–6

Here is another recipe including my beloved chorizo (maybe I have Spanish roots after all!), which is a great match for eggs. It's a delicious brunch or an easy supper dish for feeding a crowd.

30g (1¼oz) butter
2 tbsp extra-virgin olive oil
300g (11oz) red onion,
    chopped into 1cm (½in)
    dice
1 garlic clove, finely sliced
100g (3½oz) chorizo, peeled
    and diced
300g (11oz) potato, chopped
    into 1cm (½in) dice
300g (11oz) smoked
    haddock or coley, skin
    and bones removed
    and cut into 1cm (½in)
    chunks
6 large eggs, beaten
3 tbsp chopped parsley
4 spring onions, chopped
sea salt and freshly ground
    black pepper

To serve
leafy salad and crusty bread

1. Preheat the oven to 160°C (325°F), Gas mark 3 or preheat the grill.

2. Melt the butter and oil in an ovenproof frying pan. Add the onion, garlic, chorizo and potato and season with salt and pepper. Turn the heat down low, cover with a lid and allow to sweat until soft but not brown.

3. When the onions and potatoes are soft, add the smoked fish and cook for a few minutes.

4. While the fish is cooking, whisk the eggs with the chopped parsley and spring onions in a large bowl. Spoon the fish and potato mixture into the egg mixture with a slotted spoon, leaving the oil behind in the frying pan. Put the frying pan back on the heat and allow the oil to bubble but not smoke. Fold the egg, fish and potato together and season again with salt and black pepper, then pour it into the frying pan. Allow the mixture to set in the bottom of the pan, then transfer it to the oven, or put it under a medium grill, until it is cooked through.

5. Turn out the omelette onto a plate and then turn it over again onto a serving plate so that its top is facing up. Serve immediately, or at room temperature, with a leafy salad and crusty bread.

Beetroot, dill and horseradish gravlax with mustard and dill mayonnaise

SERVES 10–12, CAN BE HALVED

Gravlax dates back to the Middle Ages when Nordic fishermen would salt their salmon and ferment it by burying it in the sand above the high-tide line. The word comes from the Scandinavian *grava,* meaning 'grave' or 'to dig', and *lax,* meaning 'salmon'. These days the salmon can be cured in the fridge in just a few days – in which time the salty marinade forms a brine with the juices. While beetroot is not always used in a gravlax, I love the sweet earthiness that it brings as well as, of course, the vibrant colour. Serve this with the classic sweet-sour dill mayonnaise on my Three-Seed Pumpernickel Bread (page 200) or Rye and Sesame Bread (page 203) or with boiled potatoes.

2 raw beetroot, peeled and chopped
60g (2½oz) fine salt
30g (1¼oz) caster sugar
25g (1oz) dill, finely chopped, plus extra to sprinkle (optional)
25g (1oz) finely grated horseradish
600g (1lb 5oz) salmon fillet, wild or organic if possible, with with skin

For the mayonnaise
2 egg yolks
2 tbsp Dijon mustard
2 tsp caster sugar
3 tsp white wine vinegar or cider vinegar
2 tbsp chopped dill
150ml (5fl oz) sunflower oil
sea salt and freshly ground black pepper

1. Put the beetroot into a blender with the salt and sugar. Whiz for 10–20 seconds, then scrape down the sides of the bowl or jug and whiz again. Repeat a few times until it turns into a wet paste – it will take a few minutes. Transfer the paste to a bowl, scraping it all out. Stir in the dill and horseradish to combine.

2. Line a baking tray with cling film and place the salmon on top. Cover the salmon evenly with the beetroot mix. Wrap the salmon well in cling film, place back on the tray, then rest a chopping board or other heavy weight on top of the fish. Refrigerate for two days, turning it once or twice.

3. When you are ready to serve the gravlax, make the mayonnaise. Place the egg yolks in a glass bowl and, using a whisk, mix in the mustard, sugar, vinegar, dill and 2 pinches of salt. Continuously whisk the mixture in the bowl while adding the oil slowly in a thin, steady stream until it is completely combined to a smooth, creamy texture. (For speed, you can use an electric hand whisk.) Taste for seasoning.

4. Thinly slice the gravlax, down to the skin, but not through it, then slide the slices off the skin. Arrange the thin slices on a plate and serve with the mustard and dill mayonnaise sprinkled with dill if you like.

Shrimps with homemade mayonnaise

SERVES 4–6

This is probably our daughter Scarlett's favourite thing to eat. She can sit at a table for nearly an hour peeling and eating the little shrimps as she goes, dipping them into rich yellow mayonnaise and leaving a huge mound of the heads and shells on her plate. It's difficult to give a quantity or weight of shrimps to cook, as you may want just 10 or 12 per person, or if your guests are anything like Scarlett then you'll need to allow for about 50 each! What is important is to start with really fresh, live – if possible – shrimps for the best flavour and texture.

salt
live fresh shrimps

For the mayonnaise
2 egg yolks
1 tsp Dijon mustard
1 dessertspoon white wine
   vinegar
225ml (8fl oz) oil – I like
   to use 200ml (7fl oz)
   sunflower oil and 25ml
   (1fl oz) extra-virgin
   olive oil
sea salt and freshly ground
   black pepper

1. Fill a large saucepan with water, adding 1 tablespoon salt to 1.2 litres (2 pints) water – I always measure this, it needs to be salty. You could also use fresh sea water if you have it. Bring the salted water to the boil over a high heat, then add the shrimps and give them a quick stir. Put the lid on and bring the water back up to the boil, then boil for 2–4 minutes until the shrimps have changed from a grey-brown to a coral colour. There should be no trace of black on their heads.

2. Once cooked, drain the shrimps and spread them out on a tray to cool. If they are put into a deep bowl to cool they'll continue to cook.

3. For the mayonnaise, put the eggs in a glass bowl (a stainless-steel bowl can give the mayonnaise a grey colour). Add a pinch of salt, the mustard and vinegar, and stir to mix. Mix the oils in a jug. Continuously whisk the mixture in the bowl while adding the oil slowly in a thin, steady stream until it is completely combined to a smooth, creamy texture. Taste for seasoning. (For speed, you can use an electric hand whisk.)

4. Eat the shrimps straight away (the best result!) or pop them into the fridge, where they'll keep for a couple of days. The mayonnaise will keep, covered, in the fridge for up to a week. To eat, peel the prawns and dip them into the mayonnaise.

Quick potted shrimp or shellfish

SERVES 4

Sweet, garlicky shrimps cooked in butter then spread over warm toast is a wonderful thing and, in fact, one of my favourite meals. If you prefer, you can make this using crab, lobster or prawns.

75g (3oz) butter
1 small garlic clove, crushed with a pinch of salt
1–2 tsp chopped thyme, marjoram or parsley, to taste
200g (7oz) cooked and shelled shrimps, prawns or lobster, chopped coarsely, or crabmeat
2 tbsp lemon juice
sea salt and freshly ground black pepper

To serve
crusty bread

1. Melt the butter in a wide sauté or frying pan over a medium heat until it foams. Add the garlic and chopped herbs. Cook for 1 minute, until the garlic is a very pale golden colour, then add the shellfish, lemon juice and a little twist of black pepper, and cook for a few minutes until the shellfish has absorbed the delicious herby garlic flavours.

2. Spoon the shellfish into four little ramekins or small glasses, packing it down well, then divide the remainder of the cooking butter over the top of each to just cover. Transfer the ramekins to the fridge to allow the butter to set, then serve at room temperature with crusty bread.

Cheese, onion and bacon potato cakes

MAKES 8 POTATO CAKES (SERVES 4 AS A MAIN COURSE OR 8 AS A STARTER)

A simple and comforting brunch or supper dish, this is also lovely to make if you need to use up leftover potatoes.

30g (1¼oz) butter, plus extra for frying the potato cakes
100g (3½oz) onion, finely chopped
100g (3½oz) streaky bacon, cut into 1cm (½in) strips (lardons)
1 garlic clove, finely chopped
200g (7oz) Cheddar cheese, grated
500g (1lb 2oz) mashed potato (cold or left over)
2 tbsp chopped parsley
2 tbsp chopped green parts of spring onions (optional)
1 large egg, beaten
sea salt and freshly ground black pepper

To serve
green salad

1. Melt the 30g (1¼oz) of butter in a saucepan and add the onion. Cover the pan and allow to sweat over a gentle heat until nearly soft, then add the bacon and garlic and fry until the garlic is cooked and the bacon is golden around the edges.

2. Mix the bacon, onion and garlic mixture with all the other ingredients in a bowl and form into eight even-sized patties. Add more butter to the pan and heat until foaming, then fry the patties on each side until golden brown and piping hot. Serve with a green salad.

Kale gratin

We grow a lot of kale at Ballymaloe, and thankfully I adore it, so I'm always using it in all sorts of different ways. This is a supremely comforting gratin that is also wonderful served with a roast chicken (page 104) or a leg of lamb (page 139).

800g (1¾lb) kale with stalks on (curly kale or cavolo nero)
about 800ml (1 pint 9fl oz) milk
100g (3½oz) butter
100g (3½oz) flour
1 tsp Dijon mustard
150g (5oz) cheese, grated
pinch of grated nutmeg
sea salt and freshly ground black pepper

For the buttered crumbs
60g (2½oz) butter
120g (4oz) breadcrumbs
100g (3½oz) cheese, grated

1. Preheat the oven to 180°C (350°F), Gas mark 4.

2. Remove the kale stalks and then chop finely, then set to one side. Chop the leaves roughly and set to one side.

3. Pour 300ml (½ pint) water into a large saucepan, add ½ teaspoon salt and bring to the boil. Add the chopped stalks, cover the pan and cook for another 2–4 minutes, until tender. Add the leaves and cook again over a high heat, with the lid on, for 8–10 minutes until tender. Pour the contents of the pan into a sieve or colander sitting over a heatproof bowl – make sure to reserve all the liquid – and press the kale quite dry with a wooden spoon. Pour the liquid into a measuring jug and add enough milk to make it up to 1 litre (1¾ pints).

4. While the kale is draining, add the butter and flour to the pot. Cook over a medium heat, stirring for 2 minutes until you have a roux. Using a whisk, pour on the milk mixture, whisking all the time to avoid getting lumps. Bring to the boil, still whisking, to form a smooth, thick, creamy sauce. Take off the heat and stir in the Dijon mustard, then add the grated cheese and nutmeg and season to taste with salt and pepper. Return the drained kale to the pot, mixing it thoroughly into the sauce. Transfer to an ovenproof gratin dish.

5. Next, make the buttered crumbs. Melt the butter in a pan, add the breadcrumbs and grated cheese and stir to combine. Scatter the crumbs over the kale. (At this stage, this can be set aside and reheated later in the oven for 25–30 minutes.)

6. Place in the oven for 15–20 minutes until bubbling hot and golden on top.

Mum larking about on a cart (above) and pony (below).

Mum's cauliflower cheese

SERVES 4–6

For me, cauliflower cheese is serious comfort food. It comes with a shed-load of nostalgia, too, as I think of the round terracotta gratin dish it was always cooked in at home. It would come out of the Aga golden and bubbling, often accompanied by roast chicken.

1 cauliflower, broken into small florets, leaves reserved
sea salt and freshly ground black pepper
1 tbsp chopped parsley, to serve

For the cheese sauce
600ml (1 pint) full-cream milk
a few slices of carrot
a few slices of onion
1 sprig of parsley
1 sprig of thyme
3 black peppercorns
50g (2oz) butter
50g (2oz) plain flour
2 tsp Dijon mustard
150g (5oz) Cheddar cheese, grated
good pinch of grated nutmeg

1. First, make the cheese sauce. Pour the milk into a small saucepan and add the carrot, onion, parsley, thyme and peppercorns. Bring to the boil, then turn down the heat and simmer for 4–5 minutes. Remove from the heat and leave to infuse for 10 minutes. Strain the milk through a sieve placed over a small saucepan and bring the milk back to the boil.

2. Meanwhile, melt the butter in a saucepan over a medium-high heat, then add the flour and stir (or use a whisk) on the heat for 2 minutes to make a roux.Whisk the hot milk into the roux, a little at a time, until well blended, then leave to simmer gently for 4–5 minutes until thickened to the desired consistency. Add the mustard and most of the grated cheese, reserving a little cheese to scatter over the top of the dish, and stir until melted. Season to taste with salt, pepper and nutmeg.

3. Next, prepare the cauliflower. You will need a gratin dish large enough to hold the cauliflower florets in a single layer. Fill a large saucepan with water to a depth of 2.5cm (1in) and add a little salt. Arrange the cauliflower leaves on the bottom, sit the cauliflower florets on top, cover with a lid and bring to the boil. Cook for 8–10 minutes until the stalks are tender when pierced with a knife. Remove the cauliflower (discarding the leaves), drain well and arrange in the gratin dish.

4. Preheat the grill to high. Pour the sauce over the cauliflower in the dish and scatter with the reserved cheese. Place the dish under the grill for 2–3 minutes until golden and bubbling on top. Scatter over the chopped parsley and serve.

TIP
If reheating the cauliflower cheese from cool, place it in an oven preheated to 200°C (400°F), Gas mark 6 for 15–20 minutes until golden and bubbling hot.

Leek and Cheddar tart with rye pastry

SERVES 6

Cheese loves all the alliums, and none more so than the leek. This tart, with its crumbly shortcrust pastry that sits under the creamy leek filling, makes for a most delicious lunch.

For the rye pastry
100g (3½oz) wholemeal rye flour
100g (3½oz) plain flour, plus extra for dusting
pinch of salt
100g (3½oz) cold butter
1 egg, beaten

For the filling
25g (1oz) butter
2 tbsp extra-virgin olive oil
2 leeks, cut into 5mm (¼in) slices
3 eggs
125ml (4½floz) regular or double cream
pinch of cayenne pepper
1 tbsp chopped parsley
100g (3½oz) grated Cheddar cheese
50g (2oz) finely grated hard cheese, such as Parmesan
sea salt and freshly ground black pepper

1. You will need a 23cm (9in) tart tin with 2.5cm (1in) high sides or a 20cm (8in) quiche tin with 3.5cm (1¼in) high sides. Preheat the oven to 180°C (350°F), Gas mark 4.

2. First, make the pastry. Place both flours in a bowl with the salt and rub in the butter until it resembles coarse breadcrumbs. Add nearly but not quite all the beaten egg – enough to bring it together to a dough. Pat the dough into a round 1cm (½in) thick, wrap it in cling film or put it into a plastic bag and place in the fridge for at least 30 minutes. (It can be stored in the fridge for up to two days.)

3. Meanwhile, prepare the filling. Place the butter and oil in a saucepan over a medium heat and allow to melt and foam. Add the leeks and season with salt and pepper, tossing the leeks in the butter and oil. Turn the heat down to low, cover with a lid and cook for 6–8 minutes until softened. Set aside to cool.

4. Whisk the eggs in a bowl, add the cream, cayenne and parsley and season to taste with salt and pepper.

5. Next, return to the pastry. Dust your worktop with some flour and roll out the dough into a round 4mm (⅛in) thick, dusting the top with flour and regularly sliding a palette knife underneath the round to stop it sticking. Brush off any excess flour, then place your rolling pin on top of the pastry and drape it onto it. Hold the rolling pin over the centre of the tin and unroll the pastry into the tin. It could be quite crumbly, so work carefully. Gently ease in the pastry, pressing it into the edge around the bottom, then pinch off the excess all the way around, leaving it a little higher than the tin. Using your fingertips, pinch up the lip of the pastry to make a neat edge that's slightly taller than the tin itself. Make sure there are no cracks in the pastry case, but if there are, patch them up with leftover scraps.

6. Combine the two cheeses in a bowl and scatter half over the pastry base, to cover. Next, tip in the cooked leeks, then pour in the egg mix and scatter the remaining cheese over the top.

7. Bake in the oven for 30–40 minutes until golden brown on top and set in the centre. Remove from the oven and allow to stand for 5 minutes before removing from the tin. Serve warm or cold.

Cheesy balloons

This recipe is a savoury version of the sweet doughnut-like balloons that my husband's grandmother, Myrtle Allen, used to make for the children staying at Ballymaloe House. Ivan, my husband's cousin, came up with the brilliant idea of making them cheesy. Watch out, they're moreish.

oil, for deep-frying
150g (5oz) plain flour
½ tsp baking powder
good pinch of cayenne pepper
good pinch of salt
75g (3oz) Parmesan cheese, very finely grated (a good opportunity to use up delicious leftover cheeses that you might have hanging around)
175ml (6fl oz) milk

1. Heat the oil in a deep-fat fryer to 180°C (350°F).

2. Sift the flour, baking powder and cayenne pepper into a bowl. Mix in the salt and grated cheese. Make a well in the centre and pour in the milk, whisking all the time until you have a thick batter.

3. When the oil is hot, take a dessertspoonful of the mixture and, using another spoon, push it off gently, so that it drops as a round ball into the oil. Cook a few at a time, not overcrowding the pan or the oil will cool down and the balloons will be stodgy. Fry until deep golden, 3–4 minutes, turning them over halfway through cooking.

4. Using a slotted spoon, remove from the oil and drain on kitchen paper. Serve warm.

Crabby potato cakes with lemon and caper mayonnaise

MAKES 10–12 CAKES

A step up from your average fish cakes, these are a great way of making a little crab go a long way. If you can get hold of some of the brown meat from the crab, the flavour will go even further. I love them served with a generously herby mayonnaise.

500g (1lb 2oz) cooked crabmeat, brown and white if possible, free from any shell
500g (1lb 2 oz) cold mashed potato (leftover mash works well)
1 garlic clove, crushed
finely grated zest of 1 small lemon, plus lemon wedges, to serve
1 large egg
70g (2½oz) spring onions, finely chopped
1 tsp chopped thyme leaves
1 tbsp chopped parsley
a good knob of butter
1 tsp extra-virgin olive oil
sea salt and freshly ground black pepper

For the lemon and caper mayonnaise
2 tbsp chopped capers
2 tbsp lemon juice, plus extra to serve.
1 tsp Dijon mustard
generous pinch of salt
2 egg yolks
50ml (2fl oz) extra-virgin olive oil
150ml (5fl oz) sunflower oil

To serve
green salad

1. First make the mayonnaise. Put all the ingredients, except the oils, in a glass bowl (a stainless-steel bowl can give the mayonnaise a grey colour.) Mix the oils in a jug. Continuously whisk the mixture in the bowl while adding the oil slowly in a thin, steady stream until it is completely combined to a smooth, creamy texture. Taste for seasoning and add an extra splash of lemon juice if necessary. (For speed, you can use an electric hand whisk.) Cover and chill while you make the burgers.

2. Mix all the ingredients, except the butter and olive oil, together in a bowl and season with salt and pepper, tasting and adjusting the seasoning if needed.

3. Shape the mixture into 10 or 12 even-sized patties. Melt the butter in a frying pan with the olive oil. Fry the crab cakes on one side until golden, then turn and fry the other side. If you use an ovenproof pan, you can finish these off in the oven at 200°C (400°F), Gas mark 6, for 5–8 minutes.

4. Serve with lemon and chive mayonnaise, a green salad and lemon wedges.

Tomato, onion and Gruyère tart

SERVES 4–6

The spelt pastry in this tart delivers a gorgeous nuttiness that works perfectly with the tomato, onion and cheese. Use the best ripe, red tomatoes that you can find.

For the pastry
125g (4½oz) cold butter
250g (9oz) white spelt flour
pinch of salt
1 egg, beaten

For the onion layer
100g (3½oz) butter
1kg (2lb 3oz) onions,
   halved and sliced
4 garlic cloves, chopped
4 tsp chopped rosemary
sea salt and freshly ground
   black pepper

For the cheese layer
150g (5oz) Gruyère cheese,
   grated

For the tomato layer
300g (11oz) ripe tomatoes,
   sliced 7.5mm (⅓in) thick
little drizzle of extra-virgin
   olive oil

To serve
basil pesto or tapenade
leafy salad

1. You will need a 21cm x 31cm (8½in x 12½in) Swiss roll tin. Preheat the oven to 180°C (350°F), Gas mark 4.

2. Make the pastry by rubbing the butter into the flour and salt until it is a light, crumbly texture, then add enough beaten egg to bring it together to form a soft dough. Wrap the dough in cling film and leave to rest in the fridge for at least 30 minutes, or overnight if you like.

3. Next, prepare the onions. Melt the butter in a sauté pan over a medium heat, add the sliced onions, garlic and rosemary with a pinch of salt and a twist of pepper, cover with a lid and cook until the onions soften. Then remove the lid and allow the onions to darken and reduce for 30–40 minutes, stirring frequently so that they don't burn, until they are a nutty brown colour. Set aside.

4. Roll out the pastry into a rectangle large enough to line the base and sides of the tin and put it in the fridge to rest again while you prepare the remaining tart ingredients.

5. Once chilled, sprinkle the grated Gruyère cheese in an even layer onto the pastry shell. Then top with an even layer of the caramelised onions and place the tomato slices, slightly overlapping on top of the onion. Sprinkle with salt and a twist of freshly ground black pepper and drizzle with olive oil.

6. Bake in the oven for 40 minutes. Remove from the tray, if you can, or else cut squares and take out one at a time. Serve drizzled with pesto or tapenade and with a leafy salad for a delicious lunch.

Leek and chicken risotto

SERVES 4–6

One of the loveliest things to make using leftover roast chicken, this risotto is a family favourite. Make sure you don't overcook the rice or it will be heavy and stodgy. I love my risotto to be almost (but not quite) soupy, so that it runs out to the edges of the plate.

1.5 litres (2½ pints) chicken stock
25g (1oz) butter
3 tbsp extra-virgin olive oil
1 medium or 2 small leeks, finely chopped
500g (1lb 2oz) risotto rice, such as Arborio or Carnaroli
75ml (3fl oz) dry white wine (optional)
75g (3oz) Parmesan cheese, finely grated, plus extra for sprinkling
generous handful of shredded leftover roasted chicken
juice of ½ lemon, or to taste
2 tbsp chopped parsley
½–1 tsp chopped thyme, to taste
sea salt and freshly ground black pepper

1. Pour the stock into a pot and bring to the boil, then turn the heat down and keep it at a simmer.

2. Meanwhile, melt the butter with the olive oil in a large saucepan over a low heat, add the leeks and some salt and pepper, cover with a lid and sweat gently until soft. Add the rice and stir for a minute to coat it in the oil. Then, if you're using the wine (which I do if I have some handy), add it now, turn the heat up to medium and let the wine bubble and evaporate, which will take 2 minutes.

3. Lower the heat to medium-low, add a ladleful (about 150ml/5fl oz) of the simmering stock and stir continuously until the liquid has been absorbed, then add another ladleful and repeat the process. Keep adding the stock in this way until the rice is cooked and is loose and creamy in consistency, which should take 16–18 minutes.

4. When you're happy with the texture (you might want to add more stock), stir in the grated cheese, the shredded chicken, some lemon juice to taste, the parsley and thyme and some seasoning, if needed. Serve with more grated cheese sprinkled over the top.

Chicken Kiev

Chicken Kiev is a classic for good reason – crisp, crunchy breadcrumbs surrounding a juicy chicken breast enclosing a pocket of melted garlic butter. This version has the added bonus of lemon and Parmesan cheese, too. A firm family favourite.

4 chicken breasts, skin removed
2 garlic cloves, crushed with a pinch of salt
4 tbsp chopped parsley
75g (3oz) butter
40g (1½oz) Parmesan cheese, grated
zest and juice of 1 lemon
1 egg, beaten
3 tbsp plain flour
120g (4oz) breadcrumbs
sea salt and freshly ground black pepper

For frying
25g (1oz) butter
2 tbsp extra-virgin olive oil

To serve
leafy salad or seasonal vegetables

1. Pierce the thick end of the breasts with a thin sharp knife. Push the blade of the knife down to near the thin end of the breast, being careful not to cut right through the flesh. Sweep the blade from side to side to make the pocket wider on the inside but keeping the incision small. This will help to stop the lovely garlic butter leaking out. Set aside.

2. Add the garlic, parsley, butter and grated Parmesan to the lemon juice and mix well to combine. Divide the flavoured butter into four and stuff one piece into the pocket of each chicken breast, pushing it well down inside.

3. Put the beaten egg in a low wide dish. Mix a good pinch of salt and pepper into the flour and place in a similar dish, then add the lemon zest to the breadcrumbs and place in a third dish.

4. Toss the breasts one at a time into first the flour, then the eggs and lastly the breadcrumbs, making sure they are thoroughly coated at each stage. Set aside. Preheat the oven to 200°C (400°F), Gas mark 6.

5. To fry the chicken, put the butter and olive oil into an ovenproof frying pan and heat until foaming. Add the four breasts to the pan and fry on one side until golden brown, then turn them over and pop the pan into the oven for 10–20 minutes, depending on the size of the breasts.

6. When the chicken breasts are cooked through and golden all over, serve with a leafy salad or seasonal vegetables.

Chicken legs with basmati rice and caramelised onion and herbs

SERVES 4–6

When I was growing up, my mum was queen of the one-pot meals. This is my Indian/ Middle-Eastern version of her chicken and rice suppers. I love the convenience of a pilau – an Indian or Middle-Eastern dish of rice cooked in stock that typically has added vegetables, seafood or meat. This version has chicken legs and sweet, golden caramelised onions, which balance perfectly with the zingy lemon and oodles of fresh herbs.

2 tbsp extra-virgin olive oil
4 chicken legs, divided into
   drumsticks and thighs, if
   you wish
4 onions, sliced
4 garlic cloves, finely sliced
4 tbsp thyme leaves
350g (12oz) basmati rice
150ml (5fl oz) chicken stock
zest and juice of 1 lemon
4 tbsp chopped parsley
sea salt and freshly ground
   black pepper

To serve
green salad

1. Heat the olive oil in a flameproof casserole over a medium heat. Fry all the chicken pieces with a sprinkle of salt and pepper, turning occasionally, until golden all over. This should take 10–15 minutes to get the chicken partially cooked. Remove the chicken and set aside.

2. Put the sliced onions into the pan with the fat left from frying the chicken. Cook over a low heat for 45 minutes or until they turn a dark golden caramel colour, stirring frequently to prevent them sticking and burning.

3. Add the garlic and thyme leaves and cook for 2–3 minutes to soften slightly. Add the rice to the onions and stir to coat the rice with the oily mixture.

4. Bring the stock to the boil in a saucepan. Return the chicken to the casserole with the lemon zest, then pour in the boiling stock. Add another sprinkle of salt and pepper, cover the pan with a lid and cook over a low heat for 25 minutes or until the rice is tender and the chicken is cooked.

5. Finally, squeeze the lemon juice over and sprinkle the chopped parsley on top. Serve immediately with a large green salad.

Mum's roast chicken with lemon and herb stuffing and gravy

SERVES 4–6

Mum has always made this stuffing for a roast chicken – not that she ever used a recipe. The hint of lemon zest with all the fresh herbs makes for the most comforting and delicious meal that there is. I recommend brining the chicken beforehand as it adds so much tenderness and flavour to the meat. See page 106 for instructions on how to do this.

1 x 1.5–2.25kg (3¼–5lb) chicken
15g (½oz) butter, softened
sea salt and freshly ground black pepper

For the stuffing
25g (1oz) butter
1 tbsp extra-virgin olive oil
1 onion, chopped
1 garlic clove, finely chopped
3 tbsp mixed chopped parsley, chives, thyme, rosemary and sage
finely grated zest of 1 lemon
100g (3½oz) white breadcrumbs

For the gravy
2 tbsp plain flour (optional)
600ml (1 pint) chicken stock

To serve
Balsamic Roast Beetroot with Thyme
Buttered Leeks
Granny's Roast Potatoes

1. First, make the stuffing. Melt the butter in a saucepan with the olive oil over a medium-low heat, then add the onion and garlic. Cover with a butter wrapper or a piece of baking parchment and then a lid, and cook over a low heat for 8–10 minutes until the onions are soft but not browned.

2. Take the onions off the heat, then stir in the herbs, lemon zest and breadcrumbs, season with salt and pepper and leave to cool.

3. Preheat the oven to 180°C (350°F), Gas mark 4. Spoon the cooled stuffing into the chicken cavity and place the bird in a roasting tin. Smear the butter over the skin and sprinkle with salt and pepper. Roast in the oven for 1½–1¾ hours (allowing 20 minutes per 450g/1lb), basting occasionally, until cooked through. If the skin begins to look quite dark during cooking, cover the chicken with some foil or baking parchment.

4. To check whether the chicken is fully cooked, stick a skewer into the thigh with a spoon placed underneath to catch the juices – the juices should run clear. Also, the legs should feel quite loose on the bird. When cooked, transfer the chicken to a serving plate and leave to rest in the oven at the lowest temperature, if possible, while you make the gravy.

5. To make the gravy, pour or spoon off the remainder of the fat and save. Place the roasting tin on the hob, scatter the flour (if using) over the top and whisk in well. This will help to slightly thicken the gravy. Add the chicken stock to the roasting tin and bring to the boil, whisking all the time to dissolve the caramelised meaty bits that are stuck to the tray (these are full of flavour). If the flavour of the gravy is weak, boil it for a few minutes to concentrate the flavour. Strain, then serve in a hot gravy boat or jug.

6. Serve with Balsamic Roast Beetroot with Thyme (page 107), Buttered Leeks (page 107) and Granny's Roast Potatoes (page 109).

How to brine a chicken or a turkey

This is an age-old method for adding both moisture and flavour to the meat before roasting which has become hugely popular again. The salt water helps to keep the meat tender and juicy; you can make a basic salt and water brine, or you can add aromatics such as bay leaves, peppercorns, cloves and dried juniper berries.

sea salt
chicken or turkey
flavourings such as bay
    leaves, peppercorns,
    cloves or dried juniper
    berries (optional)

1. I use a ratio of 6 per cent salt to water for my brine, making sure there is enough water to cover the bird well. So if your bird takes 4 litres (7 pints) water to completely submerge it, then you need to use 240g (8½oz) of salt. Stir the salt into the water to dissolve it, then add the bird and place in the fridge or somewhere cool for 12–18 hours for a chicken, or 24 hours for a turkey.

2. When the brining time is up, take the bird out of the water, pat it dry thoroughly with kitchen paper and roast it in the normal way.

Balsamic roast beetroot with thyme

SERVES 4 AS A SIDE DISH

The deep earthiness of the beetroot loves the little piquant kick from the balsamic vinegar in this recipe – it's simply delicious served with roast chicken, lamb or fish.

450g (1lb) raw beetroot, peeled and cut through the root into 6 wedges
2 tbsp extra-virgin olive oil
1 tbsp balsamic vinegar
1 tbsp chopped thyme leaves
sea salt and freshly ground black pepper

1. Preheat the oven to 200°C (400°F), Gas mark 6.

2. Place the beetroot wedges in a bowl and drizzle with the olive oil, balsamic vinegar and chopped thyme. Season with salt and pepper and toss together to mix.

3. Tip onto a baking sheet in a single layer, place in the oven and cook for 30–40 minutes until tender and slightly crisp at the edges. Remove from the oven and serve.

Buttered leeks

SERVES 4–6 AS A SIDE DISH

A lovely way to cook leeks, retaining all the subtle sweet flavour and goodness.

50g (2oz) butter
4 medium-sized leeks, dark-green tops removed, white part cut into 5mm (¼in) slices
sea salt and freshly ground black pepper

1. Melt the butter in a saucepan over a medium heat and when it starts foaming add the leeks and toss gently. Add 1 tablespoon water and season to taste with salt and pepper.

2. Turn the heat right down, cover with a tight-fitting lid and cook for 5–8 minutes until tender, stirring every now and then.

Dad's mum, Sheila (Granny Mags),
and with her husband, Robert, on
their wedding day (below).

Granny's roast potatoes

SERVES 4–6 AS A SIDE DISH

My paternal grandmother was a good cook. I have many memories of all the Sunday lunches we had sitting around her dining room table with the polished silver and all the twinkling crystal. My favourite thing that she made? It's a toss up between her chewy, crisp meringues and her delicious roast potatoes. Her trick to getting the outside edges of the potatoes really good and crunchy was to shake them, once drained, in the pan with the lid on to roughen them up. I always think of her when I'm making roast potatoes.

10 large floury potatoes, cut widthways at a slight angle into halves or thirds

duck or goose fat, or beef dripping or extra-virgin olive oil

sea salt

1. Preheat the oven to 220°C (425°F), Gas mark 7.

2. Bring a large pan of salted water to the boil. Lower the potatoes into the pan and cook for 10 minutes until the outer layer of the potatoes have softened. Drain, then shake the potatoes around in the dry pan with the lid on – this roughens the surface of the potatoes and makes them crispier when roasting.

3. Heat a few tablespoons of the fat or oil in a roasting tin on the hob and toss the potatoes in it, making sure they are well coated (add more fat if they are not). Sprinkle with salt and place in the hot oven for 45–55 minutes, basting (spooning the hot oil or fat over them) every now and then and turning the potatoes over after 20 minutes or so until golden and crisp.

Grilled butterflied chicken breast with crushed potato

SERVES 4

The advantage of splitting the chicken breast so that it opens out like a book is that it cooks super-quickly, retaining lots of lovely juices inside. To ring the changes, try using rosemary or thyme or, for a warm spice note, crushed cumin and coriander. This is great with my Buttered Shoestring Courgettes (page 112).

4 skinless chicken breasts
3 tbsp extra-virgin olive oil, plus extra to serve
3 tbsp chopped herbs (dill, fennel, chervil, chives, parsley, marjoram or a mixture)
sea salt and freshly ground black pepper

For the potatoes
8–12 waxy new potatoes (2–3 golf-ball-sized potatoes per person)
2 tbsp extra-virgin olive oil
1 tbsp chopped rosemary

To serve
a squeeze of lemon
a drizzle of olive oil
Buttered Shoestring Courgettes (page 112)

1. Place the chicken breasts on a board and slice each one along its length almost all the way through from top to bottom, being careful to keep the cut very even, so that the two sides open out like a book.

2. Combine the oil, chopped herbs and salt and pepper in a bowl. Add the chicken breasts and toss to coat them evenly. Set aside to marinate for 10–30 minutes.

3. While the chicken is marinating, put the potatoes in a saucepan that fits them snugly. Just cover with water and add a good pinch of salt, then bring to the boil and boil until just tender. Drain well and put back into the pan. Pour in the oil, add the rosemary and shake the pot about to coat.

4. While the potatoes are cooking, heat two griddle pans on the hob over a low heat. When the potatoes are cooked, turn up the heat to let the pans get good and hot. Put the chicken breasts cut side down on one of the dry pans and fry until golden brown, then flip them over to cook on the other side – 5 minutes per side. Drizzle them with any excess marinade while they cook.

5. Remove the cooked potatoes one by one from the pan and slightly squash each one under the flat blade of a large knife – just a little, so that they break slightly. Place them on the other hot griddle pan, turning just once to keep them together.

6. When the chicken is golden brown and cooked through and the potatoes are slightly crispy, serve on a warm plate with a drizzle of olive oil and a squeeze of fresh lemon juice, alongside some Buttered Shoestring Courgettes.

Buttered shoestring courgettes

The trick when cooking courgettes is to sauté them briefly and until just tender. Cut into noodle-like shoestring shapes, these will cook in a flash and work wonderfully with chicken, such as the Grilled Butterflied Chicken Breast with Crushed Potato (page 110), turkey and fish.

2 courgettes
40g (1½oz) butter
sea salt and freshly ground
    black pepper

1. Slice each courgette lengthways on a mandolin with a 3mm (⅛in) julienne blade. Alternatively, using a sharp knife, slice into long strips and then into long, 3mm (⅛in) wide batons as evenly as you can.

2. Melt the butter with the salt and pepper in a saucepan over a medium heat, then add 2 tablespoons water and the sliced courgettes. Cook, tossing occasionally, for 5–7 minutes until the water has evaporated and the courgettes are tender and succulent. Be gentle so that they don't break up.

Chicken and spinach lasagne

SERVES 6–8

This is the kind of recipe that Mum often made – I loved it then and I still do. This lasagne will freeze well, by the way, for a couple of months, wrapped up tightly.

12–16 lasagne sheets, no-pre-cook if possible
50g (2oz) Cheddar cheese, grated
25g (1oz) Parmesan cheese, grated

For the filling
40g (1½oz) butter
200g (7oz) onion, finely chopped
2 garlic cloves, crushed
500g (1lb 2oz) minced chicken (dark meat has more flavour)
500g (1lb 2oz) lean minced pork
¼ tsp grated nutmeg or mace
500g (1lb 2oz) spinach, destalked
sea salt and freshly ground black pepper

For the béchamel sauce
850ml (1½ pints) milk
150ml (5fl oz) regular or double cream
1 carrot, roughly sliced
½ onion, roughly sliced
1 celery stick, roughly sliced
1 bouquet garni (2 sprigs of parsley, 2 sprigs of thyme and a small bay leaf)
70g (2½oz) butter
70g (2½oz) plain flour

1. First make the filling. Melt the butter in a sauté pan over a medium heat. Add the onion and garlic, cover the pan and cook until soft but not coloured. Add the chicken, pork, salt, pepper and the nutmeg or mace and cook until the mince is completely cooked. Taste and adjust the seasoning, then set aside.

2. Next make the béchamel sauce. Heat the milk and cream in a pot with some salt and pepper, the carrot, onion, celery and bouquet garni until it is at the simmer stage – do not let it boil. Set aside and allow it to infuse.

3. In another saucepan about the same size, melt the butter over a medium-high heat, then add the flour and stir (or use a whisk) on the heat for 2 minutes to make a roux. Strain the milk through a sieve into the roux on the heat, whisking continuously as it comes to the boil and thickens. Set aside.

4. Rinse the spinach and shake it well to get rid of nearly all the water. Put it in a saucepan and cook, uncovered, until it wilts and is nearly dry. The spinach cooks with the water left on the leaves from rinsing so there should be almost no water in the pan now. Set aside. Preheat the oven to 180°C (350°F), Gas mark 4.

5. To assemble the lasagne, mix a generous half of the béchamel sauce (600ml/ 1 pint) with the minced chicken and pork filling. Spread a thin layer of the remaining béchamel sauce in the bottom of the lasagne dish. Place a layer of pasta sheets on top and cover with one-third of the filling mixture. Place one-third of the spinach on the filling to cover evenly. Place another layer of lasagne sheets on top of the spinach and cover with another layer of filling followed by another layer of spinach. Then add another layer of pasta sheets, filling and spinach, with the last layer of pasta on the top. Pour the remaining béchamel sauce over the pasta. Combine the two cheeses and sprinkle over the top.

6. Bake in the oven for 40–60 minutes until bubbling and golden on top.

Duck legs with Puy lentils and onions

A wonderfully wintry main course that combines gloriously rich duck legs with earthy lentils and sweet golden onions.

1 tbsp extra-virgin olive oil
4 duck legs
6 onions, quartered through the core
2 garlic cloves, sliced
120g (4oz) Puy lentils
4 tomatoes, peeled and chopped (see tip)
100ml (3½fl oz) duck or chicken stock
200ml (7fl oz) red wine
pinch of sugar
sea salt and freshly ground black pepper

To serve
wilted greens or green salad

1. Preheat the oven to 240°C (475°F), Gas mark 9.

2. Heat the oil in a flameproof casserole over a medium heat. Sprinkle the duck legs with salt and pepper and fry, skin side down, until golden brown, then turn them over and cook for a further 15 minutes. Transfer to a plate.

3. Next, fry the onions in the casserole until golden around the edges, then add the garlic, lentils and tomatoes and cook for another minute or two. Add the stock and wine, bring to the boil and return the duck legs to the casserole, then season with salt, pepper and a pinch of sugar.

4. Cover the casserole with a lid, then place in the oven and cook for 1 hour– 1 hour 20 minutes until the meat comes away easily from the bone.

5. Serve with wilted greens or a large green salad.

TIP
To peel tomatoes, use a sharp knife to score a cross in the base of each one, cutting through the skin. Place the tomatoes in a bowl and cover with boiling water, and leave for 15–20 seconds. Drain and rinse in cold water, then peel off the skin – it should come away very easily.

Pan-fried duck breast with lazy glaze

SERVES 4

I'm always drawn to this deliciously easy sweet-sour duck with lazy glaze – it makes me a very happy girl. Serve with some greens such as kale or broccoli for a great Christmas or New Year dish.

4 duck breasts, with skin
sea salt and freshly ground
   black pepper

For the glaze
6 tbsp apple jelly
6 tbsp sloe gin or redcurrant
   jelly
6 tbsp duck or chicken
   stock, or use water
30g (1¼oz) butter

1. First, score the fat on the duck breasts with a small, sharp knife, being very careful not to cut into the flesh. Season the duck, then place, skin side down, in a cold, heavy frying pan. Put the pan over a low heat and allow the fat to render out of the duck and the skin to go a nice nutty brown colour. This can take 15–20 minutes. Then turn the breasts over to brown the flesh on the underside and the edges. When the duck is cooked to your taste, drain off all the fat and set the duck aside in a warm place to rest for 10 minutes.

2. Next, make the glaze. Put all the ingredients into a small saucepan over a medium heat to dissolve and bubble into a shiny glaze, then boil, uncovered, until the sauce has reduced by about one-third. Taste for seasoning.

3. Slice the duck breasts thinly, arrange on a plate and serve with the glaze spooned over.

Roast goose with cranberry and apple breadcrumb stuffing

SERVES 8–10

The Icelanders love their roast goose at Christmas time, and this fruity cranberry and apple stuffing is particularly festive. The stuffing can be made in advance and frozen, if you wish. Make sure it's thawed completely before stuffing the goose, though. Spiced Red Cabbage (page 121) and Icelandic Caramel Potatoes (page 121) compliment this dish perfectly.

1 whole goose, giblets removed (and saved for the stock, if you wish)
2 tbsp plain flour, for the gravy (optional)

For the stuffing
100g (3½oz) butter
300g (11oz) shallot, finely chopped
300g (11oz) celery, finely chopped
300g (11oz) cranberries, fresh or frozen
450g (1lb) eating apple, peeled, cored and finely diced (weigh when prepared)
1 tsp sugar
300g (11oz) breadcrumbs
2 tbsp chopped thyme
sea salt and freshly ground black pepper

1. First, make the stuffing. Melt the butter in a saucepan over a medium heat until foaming, then add the shallot and celery and season with salt and pepper. Turn the heat down to low, cover with a butter wrapper or a piece of baking parchment and the saucepan lid and cook for 8–10 minutes until the vegetables are soft and tender.

2. Remove the paper and the lid and stir in the cranberries, chopped apple and 75ml (3fl oz) water, then cover again and cook for 7–10 minutes until the fruit is cooked. The cranberries will burst and soften when they're ready. Stir in the sugar to dissolve, then tip into a bowl, add the breadcrumbs and chopped thyme and taste for seasoning. Allow the stuffing to get quite cold before you stuff the goose.

3. To prepare the goose, remove the wing tips and then the wishbone, for ease of carving. Put them into a saucepan with the giblets and the remaining giblet stock ingredients, if you are making it. Cover with 900ml (1 pint 12fl oz) of cold water and bring to the boil, then turn the heat down and simmer for 2 hours. Strain and set aside for the gravy.

4. Preheat the oven to 180°C (350°F), Gas mark 4. Season the cavity of the goose with salt and pepper and fill with the cold stuffing. Sprinkle some sea salt over the breast and rub it into the goose skin, then roast for 2–2½ hours. Take the roasting tin from the oven three or four times during the cooking and carefully pour off the excess fat into a heatproof bowl. (Store this fat in a jar in the fridge – it keeps for months and is wonderful for roasting or frying potatoes.)

For the goose giblet stock
(or you can use 900ml/
1 pint 12fl oz chicken
stock)
giblets (neck, heart and
gizzard)
1 small onion, halved
1 carrot, halved
1 bouquet garni
(1 sprig of thyme, 3 or
4 parsley stalks, a small
piece of celery)
6 or 7 peppercorns

5. To test whether the goose is cooked, prick the thigh at the thickest part. The juices which run out should be clear; if they are pink the goose needs a little longer. When the goose is cooked, transfer it to a large serving dish or another roasting tin. Turn the oven temperature down to its lowest setting and put the goose back into the oven while you make the gravy.

6. To make the gravy, pour or spoon off the remainder of the fat and save. Place the roasting tin on a hob, scatter the flour (if using) over the top and whisk in well. This will help to slightly thicken the gravy. Add the strained giblet stock, or chicken stock, to the roasting tin and bring to the boil, whisking all the time to dissolve the caramelised meaty bits that are stuck to the tray (these are full of flavour). If the flavour of the gravy is weak, boil it for a few minutes to concentrate the flavour. Strain, then serve in a hot gravy boat or jug.

7. Carve the goose and serve with the stuffing and gravy.

Spiced red cabbage

Spiced red cabbage seems to have roots everywhere from Germany and Austria to Scandinavia and the Nordic countries. While some recipes have more spice than others and a few contain dried fruit with the red cabbage and apples, there's always a perfectly balanced sweet-sour note at the end – delicious with the richer meats such as pork, goose and duck.

225g (8oz) red cabbage, cored and finely sliced
2 tsp cider vinegar
¼ tsp salt, or to taste
2 tbsp sugar
225g (8oz) cooking apples, peeled, cored and quartered

1. Put the red cabbage in a small pot and add the vinegar, salt and sugar, and then the apples. Add 75ml (3fl oz) water, cover the pot and cook over a gentle heat for 40–50 minutes until the apples have turned to mush and the cabbage is tender.

2. Taste, and adjust the seasoning.

Icelandic caramel potatoes

The Icelanders love their *brúnaðar kartöflur* at Christmas time and I've come across similar in Denmark and Sweden, too, though it's a mystery where this recipe comes from originally. However, the burnt-sugar caramel flavour works a treat with the Spiced Red Cabbage above and rich goose or duck.

12 golf-ball-sized waxy potatoes
75g (3oz) butter
3 tbsp sugar
sea salt and freshly ground black pepper

1. Boil the potatoes for 25–30 minutes until cooked through. Drain and set aside.

2. Melt the butter with the sugar in a pot and allow to bubble gently to a light nutty caramel, then add 4 tablespoons water.

3. Quarter the potatoes and add them to the caramel with a pinch of salt and pepper. Cook so that the caramel gets sticky again, coating the potatoes in it.

Pheasant casserole with tomatoes, cream and rosemary

SERVES 4–6

The combination of tomatoes, cream and rosemary works so well with a multitude of different meat and fish, and the pairing of this trio with pheasant, with its lean meat and rich gamey flavour, is no exception. This is delicious with orzo or mashed potatoes.

extra-virgin olive oil, for frying
250g (9oz) streaky unsmoked bacon, cut into 1.5cm (⅝in) chunks
2 pheasants, each jointed into 2 legs and 2 breasts
1 onion, sliced
1 garlic clove, chopped
1 x 400g tin of tomatoes, chopped
1 tsp sugar
150ml (5fl oz) regular or double cream
2 tsp finely chopped rosemary
50ml (2fl oz) chicken stock or water, if needed
sea salt and freshly ground black pepper

1. Preheat the oven to 160°C (325°F), Gas mark 3.

2. Place a flameproof casserole or a saucepan over a medium-low heat. Add a small drizzle of oil, then tip in the bacon. Allow to cook, stirring from time to time, until the bacon is golden. You may need to scrape the bottom of the casserole regularly with a flat-bottomed wooden spoon to scrape up the golden bits. When the bacon is cooked, tip it out onto a plate and place the casserole back on the heat.

3. Place the pheasant pieces skin side down into the casserole, adding an extra drizzle of oil if it's a bit dry. Brown the pieces of pheasant on both sides, seasoning with salt and pepper. Take the pheasant pieces out and place with the bacon.

4. Next, add the onion and garlic to the casserole with another drizzle of oil, if needed. Season with salt and pepper and cook for 8–10 minutes until soft and a little golden.

5. Tip in the tomatoes and the sugar and place the pheasant legs (not the breasts) and the bacon in the casserole. Bring up to a simmer, cover and place in the oven (or over a low heat on the hob if you prefer) and cook for 45–55 minutes until the legs are cooked. Take out of the oven, add the cream, the chopped rosemary and the browned breasts and continue to cook, covered, either in the oven or on the hob, for another few minutes until the breasts are cooked. If the sauce is a bit thick, you could add some stock or water to loosen it.

6. Season to taste and serve.

Pheasant with Jerusalem artichokes

SERVES 4

Jerusalem artichokes pack quite a nutritional punch, making them an ideal addition to our winter diet just when lovely wild pheasant is in season. Serve with earthy green Puy lentils (see opposite) for a complete and delicious main course.

2 pheasants, each jointed into 2 legs and 2 breasts
5 tbsp extra-virgin olive oil
2 large garlic cloves, chopped
2 tsp chopped sage or marjoram
6 Jerusalem artichokes
2 tbsp whiskey (optional)
150ml (5fl oz) pheasant or chicken stock
sea salt and freshly ground black pepper

To serve
Puy lentils (see opposite)

1. Place the pheasant legs in a shallow dish, drizzle with 1 tablespoon of the oil and scatter with the garlic, sage or marjoram and a pinch of salt and pepper. Rub the ingredients into the legs well. You can cook them straightaway or, if you like, place in the fridge overnight.

2. When you are ready to cook, preheat the oven to 160°C (325°F), Gas mark 3.

3. Place a small flameproof casserole or ovenproof pan over a high heat and allow to get hot. Pour in 2 tablespoons of the oil, then add the legs, skin side down, with some salt and pepper and cook until browned on both sides. Cover the casserole, place in the oven and cook for 15 minutes.

4. Meanwhile, peel the Jerusalem artichokes and cut into 6cm (2½in) chunks. After the legs have cooked for 15 minutes, add the artichokes to the casserole, cover and place back in the oven until the legs are cooked and the artichokes are tender – 25–35 minutes. Once cooked, take out of the oven and set aside.

5. About 5 minutes before the legs are ready, place a frying pan over a high heat to get hot. Season the skin side of the pheasant breasts with salt and pepper. Pour the remaining oil into the frying pan and add the breasts, skin side down. Allow to get deliciously brown, then turn over and cook for just 2 or 3 minutes until still a bit pink in the centre (or more cooked, depending on how you like it). Take out of the pan and keep warm for a minute.

6. Keeping the pan on the high heat, add the whiskey (if using) – it might flame if you're using a gas hob, so beware. Once it has boiled for a minute or finished flaming, add the stock and bring to the boil again. Season to taste with salt and pepper. If it's a bit weak, boil for another minute, uncovered, until the flavour is how you want it. Pour any juices from the pheasant leg pan into the sauce and season with salt and pepper, if needed.

7. Serve a pheasant leg and breast to each person with the tender juicy artichokes and some Puy lentils.

Lentils du Puy

The lovely little pebble-like lentils from Puy adore being served with the richer wintry meats, such as pheasant, goose and duck, and cooking them in stock adds another dimension to their gloriously earthy flavour.

2 tbsp extra-virgin olive oil
1 small onion, finely
    chopped
1 large celery stick, finely
    chopped
1 large garlic clove, finely
    chopped
200g (7oz) Puy lentils
400ml (14fl oz) chicken or
    pheasant stock
sea salt and freshly ground
    black pepper

1. Place a saucepan over a medium heat and add the oil, then the onion, celery and garlic. Season with salt and pepper and turn the heat down to low, then cover and cook for 8–10 minutes until the vegetables are tender and slightly golden around the edges.

2. Add the lentils and stir over the heat for a few seconds, then pour in the stock and season with salt and pepper. Bring to the boil, then cover the pan, turn the heat down to low and cook for 15–20 minutes until tender. Taste and adjust the seasoning, if needed.

Grilled pork chops with tomato and smoked paprika butter

SERVES 4–6

A simple flavoured butter is a great little embellishment, which can be made ahead and stored in the fridge for a few days, or even in the freezer for a few weeks. This tomato and smoked paprika butter also works a treat with barbecued sweetcorn or lamb. I normally use the 'sweet' smoked paprika, but feel free to use the 'hot' one if you fancy a kick. Serve with the deliciously aromatic Thyme and Walnut Oil Roasted Red Onion Halves (page 128).

4–6 large pork chops
extra-virgin olive oil, for
    frying

For the tomato and smoked
    paprika butter
100g (3½oz) butter, slightly
    soft
½ tsp tomato purée
½ tsp smoked paprika
1 tsp lemon juice
1 tsp Dijon mustard
1 tbsp chopped parsley
sea salt and freshly ground
    black pepper

To serve
crushed potatoes and wilted
    greens or salad

1. First make the tomato and smoked paprika butter. Mix all the ingredients for the butter together in a bowl. Wrap in cling film or baking parchment, roll into a log and chill in the fridge until firm.

2. Season the pork chops with salt and pepper and rub with a little oil. Heat a griddle pan and fry the chops for 5–8 minutes on each side until golden brown and cooked through.

3. Serve on warm plates with a few slices of the butter melting over them. They are delicious with crushed potatoes and wilted greens or salad.

TIP
If you have more butter than you need, roll it into a log, wrap in baking parchment and keep it in the freezer. It will last for ages.

Thyme and walnut oil roasted red onion halves

SERVES 4–6

Roasted onions are a revelation. If you haven't already tried the most simple recipe in the world – which is to throw some onions (still in their skins) into a hot oven for an hour before squeezing out the juicy sweet flesh – then I urge you to do it right now. This variation is just a step on from the basic recipe, but combining sweet red onions with aromatic thyme and earthy walnut oil is delicious. They go perfectly with Grilled Pork Chops with Tomato and Smoked Paprika Butter (page 126).

6 large red onions
50g (2oz) butter
2 tbsp walnut oil
2 tbsp chopped thyme
sea salt and freshly ground
　　black pepper

1. Preheat the oven to 180°C (350°F), Gas mark 4.

2. Halve the red onions from top to bottom down through the core and root. Place the onions, cut side up, on a roasting tin and put in the oven for 15 minutes.

3. While the onions are roasting, put all the other ingredients into a small saucepan and warm until the butter melts. Do not cook.

4. After 15 minutes, you will notice the onion layers starting to open. Divide the butter mixture between the onions evenly with a teaspoon, letting the lovely buttery mixture seep into each onion. At this point, you can either carry on cooking, or remove the onions from the oven to cook later.

5. Roast the onions for a further 45 minutes or until the flesh is soft and the cut surface starts to brown.

St Patrick's Day bacon with parsley sauce and cabbage purée

SERVES 4–6

Even though my mum is Icelandic, she got a good hold of the traditional Irish recipes too. This simple but delicious main course is a true expression of great Irish food.

900g (2lb) loin or collar of bacon, preferably with the rind still on

For the parsley sauce
300ml (½ pint) milk
a few slices of carrot
a few slices of onion
1 sprig of parsley
1 sprig of thyme
3 peppercorns
1 tbsp butter
1 tbsp plain flour
1 tsp Dijon mustard
3 tbsp chopped parsley
sea salt and freshly ground black pepper

For the cabbage purée
½ large green cabbage, such as savoy, cut into quarters, cored and finely shredded
50g (2oz) butter
75ml (3fl oz) regular or double cream

1. Place the bacon in a large saucepan, cover with cold water and bring slowly to the boil. Drain, refill the pan with fresh water and repeat. This gets rid of the salt (which appears as white froth on top of the water), so it may need to be done again, depending on how salty the bacon is. Taste the water – if it is still salty, repeat the process, otherwise turn the heat down, cover with a lid and simmer for 40 minutes (allowing 45 minutes per 1kg/2lb 3oz).

2. Once the bacon is cooked (a skewer inserted in the middle should come out easily), remove from the pan (reserving the cooking liquid) and leave to rest, covered with foil, a clean tea towel or an upturned bowl.

3. For the parsley sauce, pour the milk into a small saucepan and add the carrot, onion, parsley, thyme and peppercorns. Place over a medium-low heat and bring to the boil, then turn the heat down and simmer for 2 minutes. Remove from the heat and leave to infuse for 10 minutes.

4. Strain the milk through a sieve into a heatproof bowl. Melt the butter in the milk saucepan, add the flour and whisk over the heat for 1 minute. Gradually pour in the milk and whisk to remove any lumps. Bring to the boil and whisk over the heat until the sauce has thickened, then stir in the mustard and parsley and season to taste with salt and pepper (see tip).

5. While the bacon is resting, prepare the cabbage purée. Place the cabbage in a saucepan with the butter and 75ml (3fl oz) water. Cover and cook for 6–8 minutes until the cabbage has completely wilted. Add the cream and bring to the boil, then transfer to a blender or food processor and blitz to a smooth purée. Season to taste with salt and pepper.

6. Remove the rind from the bacon and cut the meat into thick slices. Serve with the cabbage purée and parsley sauce.

TIP
I normally add a splash of the bacon cooking water to thin out the parsley sauce if it needs it.

Simple pork stir-fry

SERVES 4

For me, a really great stir-fry has lots of different flavours, colours and textures.
This is a firm favourite in our house.

1 x 700–800g (1½–1¾lb)
pork fillet, trimmed of all
fat and sinew
75g (3oz) cashew nuts,
toasted and chopped
(see tip)
a few sprigs of coriander

For the marinade
1 tbsp soy sauce
1 tbsp oyster sauce
1 tbsp hoisin sauce
1 tbsp Chinese rice wine
1 tbsp toasted sesame oil

For the stir-fry
toasted sesame oil, for
frying
150g (5oz) carrots, halved
lengthways and sliced at
an angle
150g (5oz) spring onions,
sliced at an angle
150g (5oz) sugar snap peas
or mangetout, cut in half
at an angle
150g (5oz) oyster or shiitake
mushrooms, sliced
3 garlic cloves, thinly sliced
25g (1oz) fresh root ginger,
peeled, sliced and cut into
fine julienne
¼ red chilli, chopped or
sliced (optional)

To serve
noodles or rice

1. First, slice the pork fillet in half lengthways and then cut it into thin strips across at an angle. Combine all the marinade ingredients, then add the pork and mix well to cover. Leave to marinate while you prepare the vegetables for the stir-fry.

2. Preheat a wok by placing it over a medium-high heat for 5–10 minutes until very hot, then turn the heat up to as high as it will go Add a dash of toasted sesame oil and then add the pork along with all the marinade. Cook for about 5 minutes, shaking and stirring constantly. Then add all the vegetables with the garlic, ginger and chilli and cook for a further 5–10 minutes, depending on how hot your wok is.

3. Sprinkle with the toasted cashew nuts and coriander sprigs and serve with noodles or rice.

TIP
Tip the cashew nuts into a dry, non-stick frying pan or the wok as it is heating up and toast over a high heat for a minute or two, tossing regularly to avoid burning. Take off the heat and set aside to cool.

Creamy pork and ginger stew

SERVES 6

A deliciously comforting pork stew that has added warmth from the lashings of fresh ginger. If possible, ask for good thick pork shoulder chops, 1.5–2cm (⅝–¾in) thick. If you want a change of flavour, leave out the ginger and replace the coriander with marjoram, or simply parsley and chives.

50g (2oz) butter
900g (2lb) pork shoulder
    chops, cut into 2 or 3
    pieces, depending on size
300g (11oz) shallots, halved
    or quartered if large
4 garlic cloves, sliced
75g (3oz) fresh root ginger,
    peeled and finely grated
1 tbsp plain flour
    (optional)
750ml (1 pint 6fl oz)
    chicken or pork stock
600g (1lb 6oz) small waxy
    potatoes, halved
200ml (7fl oz) regular or
    double cream
sea salt and freshly ground
    black pepper
3 tbsp chopped coriander

To serve
cooked rice or orzo

1. Melt the butter in a flameproof casserole or pot. Add the pork and fry until golden on both sides, then remove. Add the shallots and garlic and fry until golden on the outside but not too dark. Add the ginger and fry for 1 minute, then return the pork to the pot and season with salt and pepper. Stir in the flour at this stage (if using), then cook for a further 2 minutes.

2. Add the stock and the potatoes, then bring to the boil, and simmer for 40–45 minutes until the potatoes are tender.

3. Add the cream, adjust the seasoning and let it bubble for 2 minutes. Sprinkle with chopped coriander and serve with rice or orzo.

Pan-fried lamb chops with apple and mint chutney

SERVES 4

This delicious fresh chutney that we make at the cookery school is just as at home sitting beside a hot spicy curry as it is with a plate of lamb chops. When cooking the lamb, make sure to get the pan very hot before adding the chops, so that they can get gorgeously dark brown on one side, before being cooked on the other side. A huge amount of flavour will come from the almost-charred, sweet, caramelised exterior of the meat.

8–12 lamb chops
a drizzle of extra-virgin
   olive oil
sea salt and freshly ground
   black pepper

**For the apple and mint
   chutney**
1 large cooking apple
1 large handful of mint
   leaves
50g (2oz) onion, roughly
   chopped
1–2 generous tbsp sugar
pinch of cayenne pepper

1. First, make the apple and mint chutney. Peel the cooking apple and cut it into quarters, then remove the core and chop the apple roughly. Place it in a food processor and add the mint leaves, onion, 1 generous tablespoon sugar, a pinch of salt and pepper and cayenne. Whiz it up until it is almost smooth, but still a little chunky, and taste. Add more sugar if it needs it, then set aside until you're ready to serve. This will keep in the fridge for a few hours.

2. Next, prepare the lamb chops. Remove any excess fat from the chops, but leave about 5mm (¼in) on, as this will give flavour and prevent the meat drying out. Drizzle with a little oil (enough to glaze) and black pepper. I like the pepper for this to be quite coarsely ground.

3. Place a griddle pan or a frying pan over a medium heat for 10 minutes to get really good and hot. When it's properly hot, turn up the heat, place the lamb chops in a single layer in the pan and sprinkle with a little salt. You might need to cook the lamb chops in two batches. Cook for 3 minutes on each side until deep golden brown and cooked to the level of 'doneness' that you like.

4. Serve the chops straight away or let them rest somewhere warm while you cook the others. Serve with the apple and mint chutney.

Irish stew with pearl barley

SERVES 4–6

There is no one traditional recipe for an Irish stew, as each household in the past would have had their own family recipe. It is said, however, that people in the south of Ireland would always add carrots, but people north of County Tipperary would not. Many make theirs by placing alternate layers of meat, onions, carrots and potatoes in a pot, which are then seasoned with salt and pepper, covered with water and stewed gently for 2 hours. However, searing the meat and vegetables before stewing, like we do at Ballymaloe, gives them a delicious sweet flavour.

15g (½oz) butter
2 tbsp extra-virgin olive oil or 2 tbsp lamb or mutton fat that you have put into the hot casserole or saucepan to render down
1kg (2lb 3oz) lamb shoulder, cut into 5cm (2in) cubes
12 baby onions, peeled
3 carrots, cut into thick slices at an angle or 12 small baby carrots, scrubbed and left whole
2 tbsp pearl barley
sprig of thyme
400ml (14fl oz) lamb or chicken stock, or water
8–12 potatoes, cut into chunks
1 tbsp chopped parsley
1 tbsp chopped chives
sea salt and freshly ground black pepper

1. Preheat the oven to 160°C (325°F), Gas mark 3.

2. Heat a flameproof casserole or a large saucepan with the butter and oil until hot, toss in the meat and cook for a minute on either side until it is brown.

3. Take the meat out of the pan, leaving any fat or oil and add the onions and carrots to cook for 2 minutes, then season with salt and pepper. Put the pearl barley and the meat back in. Add the thyme and stock, then season and bring to the boil.

4. Cover and cook in the oven for 30 minutes, then remove from the oven and arrange the potatoes on top of the stew. Cover and return to the oven for another 1–1½ hours until the meat is very tender.

5. When it is cooked, pour off the cooking liquid and leave it to stand for a minute. Add a cube of ice so the fat will float up to the top, then spoon the fat off and pour the juices back over the stew. Reheat the stew to serve. Add the chopped herbs and serve.

Mum enjoying some skiing with her younger sister, Kristin, and their mum, Ragga.

Butterflied leg of lamb with coriander

SERVES 8–10

Although I often cook a leg of lamb with the bone still in, if I want to infuse it with lots of spice or herby flavours I will remove the bone, i.e. butterfly it, and marinate the meat before roasting. Crushed coriander seeds will bring a deliciously warm, nutty note to the sweet lamb. This loves being paired with Roast Ratatouille with Feta (page 140).

1 leg of lamb, butterflied (bone removed – you can ask your butcher to do this, if you like)
2 tbsp coriander seeds
50ml (2fl oz) extra-virgin olive oil
2 garlic cloves, finely grated or crushed
2 tbsp chopped coriander
sea salt and freshly ground black pepper

1. Place the lamb in a roasting tin, fat side up. Using a small sharp knife, make deep incisions every 6cm (2½in) or so all over the top.

2. Next, place a dry frying pan on the heat and tip in the coriander seeds. Allow to get slightly darker in colour and toasted – between 30 seconds and 1 minute – then tip into a mortar and grind with a pestle. Place in a bowl and mix in the oil, garlic and chopped coriander, then season with salt and pepper. It should make a lovely thick paste. Rub the paste all over both sides of the lamb and set in the fridge to marinate for at least 1 hour or overnight.

3. When ready to cook, preheat the oven to 200°C (400°F), Gas mark 6. Roast the lamb for 30–50 minutes, depending on how you like it cooked. (This is equally good cooked on a barbecue.)

4. Rest the meat for 15–20 minutes after cooking, then carve into slices to serve, not forgetting to drizzle the delicious juices over the lamb.

Roast ratatouille with feta

SERVES 8–10

My take on a Provençal classic, which always reminds me of my mum as she seemed to make a version of this very regularly in the 1980s to go with roast lamb, and what a marvellous match it is. Try it with my Butterflied Leg of Lamb with Coriander (page 139). Great for entertaining a crowd.

2 red peppers
2 yellow peppers
175ml (6fl oz) extra-virgin olive oil
24 cherry tomatoes
4 red onions, each cut into 6 wedges
2 aubergines, cut into slices 5–7mm (¼–⅓in) thick
2 courgettes, cut into slices 5–7mm (¼–⅓in) thick
200g (7oz) feta cheese
30 black olives
sea salt and freshly ground black pepper

For the dressing
3 tbsp extra-virgin olive oil
1 tbsp sherry vinegar
2 tsp coriander seeds
2 tbsp chopped fresh coriander

1. Preheat the oven to 200°C (400°F), Gas mark 6. Rub the whole peppers all over with 1 tablespoon of the olive oil, place on a roasting tin and roast in the oven for 45–60 minutes until the peppers are completely tender.

2. Meanwhile, halve the cherry tomatoes across the equator and place in a bowl, then add the onion wedges. Pour 75ml (3fl oz) of the olive oil into the bowl and toss to coat the vegetables, then season with salt and pepper. Push the peppers up to one end of the roasting tin and tip the tomatoes, onions and all the oil in the bowl into the other end of the tray. Place back in the oven to roast. When the tomatoes are juicy and tender and the onions are roasted and golden, tip them out onto a large serving plate and set aside.

3. The peppers at this stage might be tender; if they are, take them out, place in a bowl and cover with cling film. Pour the juices from the tray over the tomatoes and onions. If the peppers are not yet cooked, pop them back in the oven.

4. Place a griddle pan over a high heat to get nice and hot. Meanwhile, place the aubergines and courgettes in a bowl, pour the remaining oil over them and season with salt and pepper. When the griddle pan is good and hot, place the slices in a single layer (you'll need to do this in batches) on the pan and cook for 2 minutes on either side until deep golden in colour. Take out and place with the tomatoes and onions on the plate.

5. When the roasted peppers have cooled enough for you to handle, peel off the cling film and peel and deseed the peppers. Discard the peel and seeds but keep all the juices – pour these over the other vegetables on the plate. Tear the pepper flesh into strips and arrange over the vegetables.

6. Next, make the dressing. Place the oil and vinegar in a bowl. Put the coriander seeds into a dry frying pan over a medium-high heat and cook for a minute until roasted and slightly darker in colour. Tip out into a mortar and grind with a pestle while still hot and add to the dressing. Taste for seasoning and adjust if needed.

7. Drizzle the dressing over the vegetables, crumble over the feta and scatter with the olives and chopped fresh coriander.

Slow-roast shoulder of lamb with cumin and coriander

SERVES 8–10

This is a recipe I come back to time and time again and I never seem to tire of the warm, nutty cumin and coriander with sweet, unctuous lamb shoulder. It is fabulously convenient, because once it's in the oven, you can get on with the rest of your day.

1 shoulder of lamb with the bone in
1 tbsp cumin seeds
1 tbsp coriander seeds
a few good pinches of sea salt
a few good pinches of coarsely cracked black peppercorns
a drizzle of extra-virgin olive oil

For the gravy
1 tbsp plain flour
500ml (18fl oz) lamb or chicken stock

1. Preheat the oven to 150°C (300°F), Gas mark 2. Place the lamb shoulder on a roasting tin and, using a small sharp knife, score the fat, but not through to the meat, all over in crisis-cross patterns.

2. Place a frying pan on the hob and tip in the cumin and the coriander seeds. Toss regularly and cook until the seeds are toasted, just a couple of shades darker and nice and fragrant. Take off the heat and crush using a pestle and mortar. Mix in a small bowl with the salt and pepper. Drizzle the oil all over the shoulder, then scatter over the spice mixture.

3. Cook for 4–5 hours until the meat is meltingly tender and almost falling off the bone. If the delicious exterior is not rich and golden in colour when the meat is cooked (it will depend on your oven), then take it out of the oven and turn the temperature up to 220°C (425°F), Gas mark 7. When it's hot, pop the lamb back in for 10 minutes or until it's browned.

4. Turn the oven off, transfer the lamb to another tin (keeping the lamb roasting tin for making gravy) and leave the meat to rest somewhere warm (with the oven door slightly ajar if you like) for at least 20 minutes, though it would be happy for an hour.

5. Meanwhile, make the gravy. Pour off the excess fat from the roasting tin but keep all the good juices and place the tray over a medium heat on the hob. Scatter in the flour and, using a whisk, mix the contents well. The flour will form a roux with any fat left from the lamb as well as all the delicious caramelised bits that are stuck to the tin. Cook this while whisking for almost a minute then, whisking all the time, pour the stock into the tray. Bring to the boil and season to taste with salt and pepper. If the gravy's a bit thin and needs more flavour, then boil for 2 minutes more. It should have thickened slightly. Transfer to a saucepan and reheat when needed.

6. To serve, carve the lamb into chunky shards (it won't slice into perfectly thin slices as it'll be so tender) and arrange in warm plates with the gravy over the top.

Lamb's kidneys with red wine and mushrooms

SERVES 4–6 AS A LIGHT MEAL, 3 AS A MAIN COURSE

This is the kind of quick-to-throw-together dish that I long for on cold winter nights. Served on buttered toast you have a supremely comforting supper.

55g (generous 2oz) butter
3 small garlic cloves, sliced very thinly
250g (9oz) button or chestnut mushrooms, cut in half lengthways, then each half cut into 3 wedges
6 lamb's kidneys, peeled, halved, all membranes removed, fat snipped from core, cut into 2cm (¾in) pieces
175ml (6fl oz) red wine
1 tbsp chopped parsley
sea salt and freshly ground black pepper

To serve
mashed potato, rice, or buttered toast

1. Place a wide frying pan over a high heat until hot. Add 15g (½oz) of the butter, and when it is melting and foaming, add the garlic. Cook briefly until soft but not yet golden, then tip in the mushrooms, season with salt and pepper and fry until golden. Tip the mushrooms and garlic onto a plate and place the pan back on the heat to get hot again.

2. Place 25g (1oz) of the butter in the pan and again allow to melt and foam, then tip in the kidney pieces and fry on all sides until a deep golden. Season with salt and pepper.

3. Add the red wine and allow to bubble and boil until it tastes more mellow and mild. Whisk in the remaining butter to form a glaze, then return the mushrooms and garlic to the pan with the parsley.

4. Serve with mashed potato or rice, or with buttered toast on the side.

Steak and kidney pudding

A supremely comforting and rib-sticking kind of dish, this is one for a cold, blustery day.

For the pastry
300g (11oz) plain flour
1 tsp baking powder
pinch of sea salt
150g (5oz) suet
2 eggs, plus 1 beaten egg
a very small splash of milk

For the filling
15g (½oz) butter
175g (6oz) onions, cut into
  1cm (½in) dice
1 garlic clove, chopped
25g (1oz) plain flour
350g (12oz) stewing beef,
  cut into 2.5cm (1in)
  chunks
175g (6oz) kidneys, peeled,
  halved, all membranes
  removed, fat snipped
  from core, cut into 2.5cm
  (1in) pieces
100ml (3½fl oz) stock,
  preferably beef
sea salt and freshly ground
  black pepper

To serve
mashed or boiled potatoes
  and vegetables

1. First make the pastry. Sift the flour and baking powder into a mixing bowl with a pinch of salt. Cut the suet into small pieces, or pulse in a food processor to chop, and rub it into the dry ingredients until it resembles coarse breadcrumbs. Whisk the 2 eggs in a bowl, add to the flour and mix to bring the dough together. You may need a teaspoon or two of water if it's not coming together. Pat the pastry into a round, 2cm (¾in) thick, cover and place in the fridge to rest for 30 minutes – or leave overnight.

2. To make the filling, melt the butter and add the onions, garlic, salt and pepper. Cover and allow to sweat over a gentle heat until soft but not coloured. Remove from the heat to cool.

3. Put the flour in a bowl with a generous pinch of salt and pepper and mix well. Toss in the beef and the kidneys, add the cooled sweated onion and garlic and mix well to coat.

4. Line a 900g (2lb) Pyrex or ceramic pudding dish with roughly ¾ of the pastry rolled out to at least 5mm (¼in) thick and spoon in the filling, then pour in the stock. Combine the beaten egg and milk to make an eggwash and brush over the edges of the pastry. Roll the remaining ¼ of the pastry out to the same thickness as the base and place it on top as a lid, sealing it well with the prongs of a fork pressed across the edge. Trim off any excess pastry around the edge.

5. Cover the top of the pudding with a sheet of baking parchment with a 4cm (1½in) folded pleat in the middle to allow for expansion, and secure with string around the top of the bowl.

6. Put the bowl inside a pan filled with boiling water that comes halfway up the side of the bowl. Put the lid on the pan, bring to the boil and simmer for 4 hours, topping up with water as necessary.

7. Preheat the oven to 150°C (300°F), Gas mark 2. Remove the pudding from the pot of water and gently peel off the baking parchment lid. Transfer the pudding to the oven for 30 minutes to crisp up the top of the pastry. Remove the pudding from the oven and allow it to stand for 5 minutes, then turn it out onto a plate with a high rim. Allow it stand a further 5 minutes before cutting into it. Serve with mashed or boiled potatoes and vegetables.

My mum, Hallfridur, as a little girl posing in her Icelandic woolen cardigan.

Beef stroganoff

SERVES 6–8

Mum has always made a mean stroganoff. I remember when we were little she would make a huge pot of it when entertaining, which always meant there'd be plenty left over, which my sister and I adored with rice or creamy mashed potato.

50g (2oz) butter
1 large onion, quartered and sliced
4 garlic cloves, sliced
good handful of mixed dried mushrooms
3 tbsp extra-virgin olive oil
1–2 tsp Dijon mustard, to taste
a grating of nutmeg
1 tsp smoked paprika
200g (7oz) sour cream
1kg (2lb 3oz) fillet of beef, trimmed and cut into strips
2 tbsp chopped parsley or chives
sea salt and freshly ground black pepper

For the roux
25g (1oz) butter
25g (1oz) plain flour

To serve
rice or mashed potato

1. First, make the roux. Melt the butter in a saucepan over a medium-high heat, add the flour and stir (or use a whisk) on the heat for 2 minutes, then set aside.

2. Now start the stroganoff. Melt the butter in a saucepan over a low heat, add the onion and garlic, cover the pan and sweat until the onion is soft but not coloured.

3. While the onion sweats, put the dried mushrooms in a jug or small heatproof bowl and pour over 250ml (9fl oz) boiling water. Allow them to rehydrate for 15 minutes.

4. When the onion is soft, remove the mushrooms from the bowl and squeeze out any water. Make sure you keep the water the mushrooms were soaked in. Slice the mushrooms if they're large, then add the mushrooms to the onion with 1 tablespoon of the oil, the mustard, nutmeg, paprika, salt and pepper. Turn up the heat and cook for 5 minutes.

5. Pour in the soaking water from the mushrooms, taking care to leave any grit from the mushrooms behind in the bottom of the jug or bowl. Then, add the cream and allow it to bubble up. Whisk in the roux and allow it to thicken.

6. Toss the beef in the remainder of the oil with some salt and pepper. In a separate large pan, fry the beef over a high heat until just browning. Add the creamy mushroom sauce and allow to bubble for a few minutes to finish cooking the beef.

7. Sprinkle with the parsley or chives and serve with rice or mashed potato.

Scandi meatballs with cream sauce

SERVES 4

Traditionally served at buffets, smorgasbords or at midsommar (midsummer) celebrations, meatballs or, as the Swedes know them, *köttbullar*, vary slightly from family to family and town to town. While opinions may differ on whether to use beef, veal or a mixture of beef and pork, with a thick sauce or a thin gravy, *köttbullar* are always accompanied by a generous dollop of lingonberry jam. Use a cranberry or redcurrant sauce if you can't get hold of any lingonberries.

30g (1¼oz) butter, plus extra for frying
1 onion, finely chopped
30g (1¼oz) crustless white bread (stale bread is good)
75ml (3fl oz) milk
500g (1lb 2oz) minced beef and pork, mixed (250g/9oz of each)
½ tsp ground allspice
¼ tsp grated nutmeg
2 tsp chopped sage
sea salt and freshly ground black pepper

For the sauce
15g (½oz) butter
2 tbsp plain flour
175ml (6fl oz) regular or double cream
175ml (6fl oz) chicken stock
juice of ¼–½ lemon, to taste

To serve
lingonberry jam or cranberry sauce

1. Melt half the butter in a saucepan over a medium heat, then add the onion and season with salt and pepper. Turn the heat down to low, cover and cook for 8–10 minutes until completely tender. Take off the heat and set aside to cool.

2. While the onion is cooking, break up the bread, place in a small bowl and cover with the milk. Leave to stand for 10 minutes or so, to absorb all the milk.

3. Place the minced meat in a bowl, add the allspice, nutmeg and sage, then season with salt and pepper and mix well. Place a frying pan on the heat and allow to get almost hot. Break off a small piece of the mixture and fry it in a little butter, then taste it and adjust the seasoning if needed.

4. Shape the mixture into 24 balls, about the size of a walnut in its shell. Cover and place in the fridge overnight, if you wish.

5. When ready to cook, place a large frying pan over a high heat, add the remaining butter and allow it to melt and foam. Tip in the meatballs and cook for 10–12 minutes, turning the heat down slightly once they are a good golden colour. When they are cooked in the centre, transfer them to a dish to keep warm.

6. To make the sauce, add the butter to the pan the meatballs were cooked in and, using a whisk, stir all the lovely juicy bits stuck to the bottom of the pan. Add the flour and continue whisking for a further 10–20 seconds. Gradually pour in the cream and stock, whisking all the time to prevent it going lumpy, and bring to the boil, then boil for 1 minute. Taste and add lemon juice and seasoning.

7. Place the meatballs on warm plates, pour over the hot cream sauce and serve with lingonberry jam or cranberry sauce.

Jarret de bœuf en daube
(Shin of beef stewed in wine)

SERVES 6

Wonderful old friends of ours, Jasper, Tiffany and Felix, have a mother who, as well as being a fabulous individual, also happens to be one of the most incredible cooks I know. Julia Wight has always been passionate about the food of Italy and France and thankfully has passed on her love of all things gastronomic to her children. This robust beef and red wine stew is one of her recipes that Jasper makes regularly.

120–170g (4–6oz) bacon or salt pork, cut into small cubes
1 tbsp extra-virgin olive oil
1 large onion, sliced
1.3kg (3lb) shin of beef, membrane and excess fat removed, cut lengthways into thick pieces
2 garlic cloves, sliced
parsley, thyme and a bay leaf, tied together with a piece of thread
175–225ml (6–8fl oz) red wine
175–225ml (6–8fl oz) beef stock or water
1–2 tsp salt

1. Preheat the oven to 140°C (275°F), Gas mark 1.

2. Place the cubes of bacon or salt pork into a heavy flameproof casserole with the oil over a medium heat. When the bacon fat runs, add the sliced onion and then arrange the beef shin pieces on top. Add the garlic and the bunch of parsley, thyme and bay.

3. Pour the red wine into a separate pan, bring it to the boil, then allow it to boil for 3–4 minutes. Add the stock or water and allow it to come to the boil again, then add the salt. Pour the wine/stock into the other pot with all the other ingredients and cover with baking parchment or foil and a lid.

4. Transfer the pot to the oven and cook for 3 hours. If your oven is too small to fit the pot, you can simmer the stew over a low heat on the hob instead. If you like, you could also cook the stew for 90 minutes one day and finish cooking it the next day at the same low heat, as wine stews improve and mature with reheating.

5. There will be plenty of delicious sauce in this stew when you serve, perfect for mopping up with potatoes or bread.

French beans with shallots and sherry vinegar

SERVES 4–6 AS A SIDE DISH

Ivan, my husband's cousin, grew up down the road from Isaac. He always loved French beans as a child and this is his way of cooking them. When teamed with a steak or some lamb chops, they'll be the most delicious beans you'll ever have tasted.

300g (11oz) French beans, trimmed
25g (1oz) butter
1 tbsp extra-virgin olive oil
50g (2oz) shallots, finely sliced into half rings
1½ tsp sherry vinegar
sea salt and freshly ground black pepper

1. Half-fill a pot with water, add a pinch of salt and bring to the boil. Add the beans and boil for 5–7 minutes until just tender.

2. Drain the beans through a sieve or colander and return the pot to the heat. Add the butter and allow it to melt and foam, then add the oil.

3. Next, add the shallots with the vinegar and cook over a medium-high heat for 1–2 minutes.

4. Return the beans to the pot with a little salt and pepper and toss them about to coat well with the shallot butter.

5. Season to taste, then serve immediately with meat, fish or chicken.

Biscuit-tin-smoked fish

SERVES 4

Smoking is addictive. When you start experimenting with a leftover biscuit tin, a few wood shavings and anything from a piece of fish to duck or chicken, you'll be amazed at just how easy and delicious this age-old method of cooking is.

Per person: 175g–200g (6–7oz) portions of filleted fish, such as pollock, cod, hake, haddock, salmon or mackerel
sea salt

1. Place the fish fillets, skin side down, on a plate. Sprinkle the flesh side of the fish with 50g (2oz) salt (so that each 200g/7oz portion should get scattered with 10g/scant ½oz salt). Leave in the fridge for 15–20 minutes. Rinse the salt off the fish well with cold water, pat dry and leave to stand and dry for another 15–20 minutes.

2. Place a handful of wood shavings (such as apple, cherry or oak) on foil in the bottom of your smoker – or in a biscuit tin with a wire rack sitting in it.

3. Place the fish, skin side down, on the rack and place the lid on top. Put it on a hob over a medium-high heat and leave for a few minutes until it is hot (it'll be smoking inside). Turn the heat down to low and continue to smoke for 8–12 minutes depending on the thickness of the fish. Once it's ready it will look just opaque inside. Take it out of the tin and use straightaway, or let it cool.

Variation – duck breast

1. Do exactly the same as in the fish recipe but first score the duck breast skin in a criss-cross pattern.

2. Place the duck breast skin side up while salting, drying and smoking. This will take 20 minutes to smoke.

Variation – chicken breast

Exactly the same as for the duck breast.

Beech
Birch
Chicory

Biscuit-tin-smoked fish with lemon cream sauce and Ulster champ

SERVES 4

The full-on flavour of the smoked fish is pleasantly eased by the lemon cream sauce and the sweet pea-and-potato mash. Champ is a traditional Irish potato dish that is supremely comforting and always reminds me of the mashed potatoes and boiled peas I loved as a child. For the best mashed potato, use a 'floury' variety, such as Golden Wonder or Kerr's Pink. For maximum goodness and flavour, peel them after boiling.

4 x 175–200g (6–7oz) fillets of white fish, hot smoked (see page 152)

For the lemon cream sauce
200ml (7fl oz) regular or double cream
juice of 1 lemon

For the Ulster champ
1kg (2lb 3oz) floury potatoes unpeeled and scrubbed
200ml (7fl oz) milk, or 150ml (5fl oz) milk and 50ml (2fl oz) single or regular cream
175g (6oz) peas
50g (2oz) spring onions, finely sliced
25g (1oz) butter
sea salt and freshly ground black pepper

1. First make the champ. Fill a saucepan with water, then add the potatoes and a good pinch of salt. Bring to the boil for 10 minutes, then pour all but about 4cm (1½in) of the water out of the pan and continue to cook the potatoes on a very low heat. (Don't be tempted to stick a knife into them as the skins will break and they will disintegrate.)

2. Cook for another 20–30 minutes until a skewer goes in easily. Drain the potatoes, peel while still hot and put into a bowl to mash by hand, or use the paddle attachment in an electric food mixer, until they are free of lumps.

3. When the potatoes are nearly cooked, place the milk (or milk and cream) in a saucepan and add the peas and spring onions. Bring to a gentle boil and simmer for 2 minutes until the peas are cooked. Set aside while you mash the potatoes. Add the butter and some salt and pepper to the potatoes, then add the hot milk (reheat if necessary) with all the peas and spring onions and mix well. Make sure to mash the potatoes completely before adding any milk. (You might not need all the milk/cream, or you might need a little more – it depends on how dry the potatoes are.) Taste for seasoning.

4. While the fish is smoking, make the sauce. Pour the cream into a saucepan and bring to the boil. Boil, uncovered, for 1 minute, then add the lemon juice and season with salt and pepper. Boil for another few minutes until it has thickened slightly, then taste for seasoning and set aside until you are ready to serve the fish.

5. Place the hot-smoked fish on warm plates and drizzle the reheated sauce over it and serve with buttery Ulster champ.

Mussels with tomato, chorizo, sherry and parsley

SERVES 4–6

I'm very grateful for the fact that we had a good varied diet growing up at home, and mussels were one of the things that I loved to eat. This is a wonderful dish, inspired by the holidays we had in Spain when I was a child.

2kg (4¼lb) mussels in their shells
2 tbsp extra-virgin olive oil
200g (7oz) chorizo, peeled and diced
2 shallots, finely chopped
2 garlic cloves, chopped
600g (1lb 5oz) very ripe tomatoes, peeled, deseeded and chopped (see tip, page 114)
60ml (2½fl oz) dry Fino or Manzanilla sherry (optional)
4 tbsp parsley, chopped

To serve
crusty bread

1. Wash the mussels very well in the sink with lots of fresh running water. Discard any open mussels or any that are not tightly shut and don't close when tapped, or ones with broken shells. Pluck off any visible beards – the fibrous tufts sticking out on the flat side between the two shells. Set the mussels aside in a bowl in the fridge.

2. Heat the oil in a saucepan large enough to hold all the mussels. Add the chorizo and fry a little but do not allow to get too dark. Next, add the shallots and garlic and cook for a few minutes, then add the tomatoes and sherry (if using) and, finally, the mussels. Put the lid on and turn the heat up to high. Shake the pot from time to time and cook until the mussels have opened – about 5 minutes.

3. When all the mussels have opened (discard any that remain closed), sprinkle with the parsley and divide among the bowls. Serve with crusty bread.

Seafood stew

SERVES 4–6

A delicious summery meal using the catch of the day. Every cook needs a great seafood stew recipe up their sleeve! I love to include a selection of different fish and shellfish, but just use what's freshest and best, and make sure not to overcook the stew after the seafood has gone in.

12–18 mussels in their shells
2 tbsp extra-virgin olive oil
1 large red onion, sliced
1 fennel bulb, sliced (keep the fronds for garnish)
2 garlic cloves, chopped
6 large very ripe tomatoes, peeled and chopped (see tip, page 114)
generous pinch of sugar
500ml (18fl oz) fish stock
500g (1lb 2oz) new potatoes, cooked, halved or quartered (waxy potatoes are best for this)
750g (1lb 10oz) assorted skinned, boneless fish (cod, hake, pollock, haddock, salmon, squid rings, etc.)
12–18 raw prawns, heads off and deveined (see tip)
1 heaped tbsp chopped herbs (such as fennel, parsley, dill, chives, marjoram, basil)
sea salt and freshly ground black pepper

To serve
leafy salad and crusty bread

1. Wash the mussels very well in the sink with lots of fresh running water. Discard any open mussels or any that are not tightly shut and don't close when tapped, or ones with broken shells. Pluck off any visible beards – the fibrous tufts sticking out on the flat side between the two shells. Set the mussels aside in a bowl in the fridge.

2. Heat the oil in a wide saucepan over a gentle heat. Add the onion, fennel and garlic with a little salt and pepper, then cover the pan and sweat until soft but not coloured. Add the tomatoes with a little more salt and pepper and the sugar. Simmer for 10–15 minutes to form a nice base for the stew. Add the fish stock and cooked potatoes and bring to the boil, then turn the heat down and simmer for a further 5 minutes.

3. Meanwhile, cut the fish into 4–5cm (1½–2in) chunks. Arrange the fish and the shellfish evenly in the stew, cover again and simmer for 5–7 minutes until the fish turns opaque and the mussels are open. Discard any mussels that remain closed.

4. Sprinkle with chopped herbs, then transfer to a large serving dish, being careful not to break up the pieces of fish. Serve with a leafy salad and crusty bread.

TIP
First, devein the prawn. Remove the head, if it's not already off, then pinch the end of the tail and ease it away from the prawn, so that, hopefully, the vein comes away with the end piece of the tail. Next, peel the prawn.

Halibut in garlic breadcrumbs

SERVES 6

Meaning 'the holy fish', halibut was often reserved for Catholic holy days. This incredibly delicious and oh-so-simple recipe comes from Julia, Jasper and Tiff's mum and is much more than the sum of its parts. Use only the freshest fish possible.

225g (8oz) butter, plus extra for greasing
225g (8oz) fresh or frozen white breadcrumbs
150ml (5fl oz) dry vermouth
2 garlic cloves, crushed or finely grated
1.1kg (2lb 6oz) halibut fillets, skinned and cut into 5cm (2in) pieces (allow 175g/6oz fish per person)
sea salt and freshly ground black pepper

To serve
green salad

1. Preheat the oven to 180°C (350°F), Gas mark 4. Line a dish into which all the fish will fit in an even layer with baking parchment, then butter the parchment.

2. Melt half the butter, then place in a bowl with the breadcrumbs, vermouth and garlic and mix. This will produce a moist paste. Spread half this in the dish, then arrange the cubes of fish on top quite close together and season with salt and pepper, then cover with the remaining paste. Melt the remaining butter and pour it over the top as evenly as possible.

3. Bake in the oven for 25 minutes, or a little less if you see that the fish is cooked. Preheat the grill. Brown under the grill and serve with a green salad.

Smoked haddock, black pudding and leek gratin

SERVES 4

A big, hearty gratin that's a meal in a dish, this uses smoked haddock, but any other smoked fish will work well, too, such as salmon or the inexpensive coley.

350g (12oz) potatoes, cut into 5mm (¼in) slices
a tiny pinch of grated nutmeg
1 sprig of thyme
1 garlic clove, crushed
250ml (9fl oz) regular or double cream
125ml (4½fl oz) milk
25g (1oz) butter
250g (9oz) smoked haddock, cut into 1cm (½in) pieces
175g (6oz) leeks, sliced into 5mm (¼in) half rings
125g (4½oz) black pudding, quartered lengthways then cut into chunks
sea salt and freshly ground black pepper

To serve
green vegetables or green salad

1. Start by putting the potato, nutmeg, thyme, garlic, cream and milk in a saucepan with a pinch of salt and pepper. Cover and bring up to a gentle simmer, then set aside to infuse.

2. Preheat the oven to 180°C (350°F), Gas mark 4.

3. Melt the butter in a frying pan over a medium heat. Add the fish, leeks and black pudding and sweat gently to soften for 8–10 minutes, then season with salt and pepper.

4. Transfer the fish mix to a 1 litre (1¾ pint) pie dish. Remove the sprig of thyme from the potato and layer the discs of potato over the fish mix in the pie dish. Pour the creamy milk from the saucepan over the potato and fish. Bake in the oven for 40–45 minutes until golden on top and bubbling.

5. Serve with green vegetables or a green salad.

Pan-fried fillet of salmon with capers, fennel and Dijon butter

SERVES 4

The rich oiliness of salmon loves flavours that have a bit of gusto, and this caper, fennel and Dijon butter works a treat. It would also be great served with barbecued or pan-fried lamb chops.

4 x 180g (6½oz) thick fillets of salmon, deboned and descaled (cut from the top of the fish so that they are fatter if possible)
1 tbsp extra-virgin olive oil
sea salt and freshly ground black pepper

For the butter
50g (2oz) softened butter
4 tsp chopped fennel fronds
1½ tsp Dijon mustard
1 tbsp roughly chopped capers

To serve
crushed potatoes and green salad

1. First, mix all the butter ingredients together and season with pepper. Scoop out and place on a sheet of cling film or baking parchment and roll into a log. Put in the fridge to firm up.

2. Put a pan with an ovenproof handle on the hob over a high heat. Brush the salmon fillets with oil and sprinkle with salt and black pepper. When the pan is hot, place the fillets of fish flesh side down and fry for 4–5 minutes until they are a golden brown. Sear the sides of the fillets if they are thick enough, then turn and fry the fish skin side down, turning the heat down to medium and continuing to cook for a further 5–8 minutes, depending on how you like them cooked.

3. Place thin slices of the butter on top of the fish and serve with crushed potatoes and a green salad.

Lentil-stuffed butternut squash

SERVES 4

When you scoop the seeds out of the butternut squash, it makes a lovely little bowl in which to roast the delicious lentil mixture. The pesto is surprisingly good – sometimes I prefer it to the classic basil version. This recipe makes one jarful, so use the rest with pasta, over roasted vegetables, with barbecued or grilled meats, in a salad or on simple crostini or bruschetta with roast peppers and cheese. If you like, replace half the parsley with mint, coriander, rocket, wild garlic leaves … The possibilities are endless.

1 very large butternut
squash
4 tbsp extra-virgin olive oil,
plus extra for drizzling
100g (3½oz) fresh
breadcrumbs

For the lentil stuffing
3 tbsp extra-virgin olive oil
100g (3½oz) celery, finely
chopped
100g (3½oz) carrot, finely
chopped
100g (3½oz) onion, finely
chopped
2 fat garlic cloves, finely
chopped
100g (3½oz) mushrooms,
finely chopped
100g (3½oz) Puy lentils
200ml (7fl oz) vegetable stock
sea salt and freshly ground
black pepper

For the parsley pesto
25g (1oz) parsley, chopped
25g (1oz) Parmesan cheese,
freshly grated
25g (1oz) pine nuts
2 garlic cloves, crushed
75ml (3fl oz) extra-virgin
olive oil

To serve
leafy salad

1. First, make the stuffing. Heat the oil in a pot, add the celery, carrot, onion and garlic and season with salt and pepper. Cover the pan and cook over a medium heat until the vegetables are soft. Remove the lid, add the mushrooms, turn up the heat and cook, uncovered, for 10–15 minutes. Next, add the lentils and stock, replace the lid and bring to a gentle simmer. Cook for 20 minutes or until the lentils are cooked. Preheat the oven to 180°C (350°F), Gas mark 4.

2. While the lentils are cooking, halve the butternut squash lengthways and scoop out the seeds. Drizzle the inside of each half with oil, season with salt and pepper and cook in the oven until just tender, 30–40 minutes.

3. Mix the breadcrumbs with the 4 tablespoons oil and set aside.

4. When the lentils are just cooked, remove the lid, turn up the heat and cook off any remaining liquid. Spoon the lentil mixture into the cavities of the squash halves – there will be enough to fill each half in a generous mound. Pat the breadcrumbs over each mound of lentils by hand, pressing down gently to keep in place. Return to the oven for 20–25 minutes until heated right through and the crumbs are browned and crispy.

5. While the lentils and squash are cooking, make the parsley pesto. Put all the ingredients except the oil, with a pinch of salt, into a food processor and whiz up. Add the oil and a pinch of salt and taste.

6. When the squash are ready, cut each half lengthways into four equal slices. Serve each person two slices of stuffed butternut squash with some leafy salad on the side and some parsley pesto. Pour any leftover pesto into a jar, cover with 1cm (½in) of oil and store in the fridge.

Roast vegetable and chickpea stew

SERVES 4

I have a real fondness for the chickpea. Whiz it up in a hummus, cook it with garlic, chorizo and chard in a broth, or include it in a chunky roasted vegetable stew to add body and extra goodness. This stew freezes well.

150g (5oz) red onion, cut through the core into 6–8 wedges
175g (6oz) sweet potato, cut into 2.5cm (1in) chunks
175g (6oz) cauliflower florets, cut into 2.5cm (1in) chunks
2 tbsp extra-virgin olive oil
100g (3½oz) onion, quartered and sliced
2 garlic cloves, chopped
pinch of dried chilli flakes or ¼–½ fresh chilli, to taste, deseeded and chopped
1 tsp cumin seeds, toasted and ground (see tip)
1 x 400g tin of tomatoes
generous pinch of sugar
1 x 400g tin of chickpeas, drained and rinsed
2 tbsp chopped coriander
sea salt and freshly ground black pepper

To serve
natural yoghurt, rice and lime wedges

1. Preheat the oven to 200°C (400°F), Gas mark 6.

2. Put the red onion, sweet potato and cauliflower florets on a baking tray, sprinkle with 1 tablespoon of the oil and toss well to coat. Roast in the oven for 20–30 minutes until golden and caramelising at the edges.

3. Put the sliced onion into a pot with the remaining oil, add the garlic and chilli and season with a little salt and pepper. Cover with a lid and sweat on a gentle heat until soft but not coloured. Add the ground cumin to the onions along with the tomatoes and simmer until the tomatoes are cooked – 10–15 minutes. Add the sugar and chickpeas and continue to cook for a further 5–10 minutes.

4. Finally, add the roasted vegetables and chopped coriander, stir and allow to bubble for a minute.

5. Serve each portion topped with a blob of natural yoghurt, with rice and wedges of lime.

TIP
To toast seeds, place in a non-stick pan over a medium-high heat and cook for a minute or so, tossing once or twice, until slightly darker in colour. Tip the toasted seeds into a mortar and crush with a pestle until fine, or place in a plastic bag and crush with a rolling pin instead.

Risotto with walnut pesto and goat's cheese

SERVES 4–6

A really simple-flavoured risotto, this relies on great-tasting walnuts. I love my risotto to be almost (but not quite) soupy in consistency – it should start to run out to the outsides of your plate.

1–1.2 litres (1¾–2 pints) chicken stock, or vegetable stock (for vegetarians)
50g (2oz) butter
4 tbsp extra-virgin olive oil
500g (1lb 2oz) onions, finely chopped
4 garlic cloves, chopped
500g (1lb 2oz) risotto rice, such as Arborio, Carnaroli or Vialone Nano
75ml (3fl oz) dry white wine
150g (5oz) soft goat's cheese
sea salt and freshly ground black pepper

For the walnut pesto
50g (2oz) walnuts
3 tbsp walnut oil
2 tbsp chopped marjoram (or parsley if you can't get marjoram)

To serve
rocket salad

1. First, make the pesto. Preheat the oven to 180°C (350°F), Gas mark 4. Put the walnuts on a baking tray and toast in the oven for 6–8 minutes (or you can do this in a dry pan on the hob, taking care not to let them get dark). Crush the walnuts finely using a pestle and mortar or the bowl of a food mixer. Stir in the walnut oil and chopped marjoram and add a pinch of salt and pepper.

2. Now make the risotto. Pour the stock into a pot and bring to the boil, then turn the heat down and keep it at a simmer.

3. Melt the butter with the oil in a wide sauté pan over a low heat. Add the onions and garlic with some salt and pepper, cover the pan and sweat over a medium-low heat until soft but not coloured.

4. Add the rice and cook, stirring regularly, until the rice is coated with oil and starting to turn translucent. Add the wine and cook until absorbed into the rice. Add a ladleful (about 150ml/5fl oz) of the simmering stock and stir continuously until the liquid has been absorbed, then add another ladleful and repeat the process. Keep adding the stock in this way until the rice is al dente, then add a final ladleful of stock and stir well.

5. Add the goat's cheese in blobs and fold it through the risotto. Divide among warm bowls, add a drizzle of walnut pesto to each and serve with a rocket salad.

Tomato risotto with lemon and basil mascarpone

SERVES 4–6

Tomatoes and rice are one of the great food matches and I love pairing them in this simple risotto, which makes a gorgeous summer starter.

1–1.25 litres (1¾–2¼ pints) vegetable stock
50g (2oz) butter
4 tbsp extra-virgin olive oil
500g (1lb 2oz) onions, chopped
4 garlic cloves, chopped
500g (1lb 2oz) risotto rice, such as Arborio, Carnaroli or Vialone Nano
75ml (3fl oz) dry white wine
500g (1lb 2oz) very ripe tomatoes, whizzed in a blender and sieved to remove seeds and skin
2 tbsp tomato purée
good pinch of sugar
sea salt and freshly ground black pepper
grated Parmesan cheese, to serve

For the lemon and basil mascarpone
4 tbsp mascarpone
4 tsp chopped basil
2 tsp lemon juice

1. Pour the stock into a pot and bring to the boil, then turn the heat down and keep it at a simmer.

2. Meanwhile, melt the butter with the oil in a large saucepan over a low heat, add the onions and garlic with some salt and pepper, cover with a lid and sweat gently until soft but not coloured.

3. Add the rice and stir well to coat it in the oil, then allow to cook for a few minutes until the grains of rice start to look translucent. Add the white wine, turn up the heat to medium and let the wine bubble up and be absorbed. Add the tomatoes, tomato purée and sugar.

4. Add a ladleful (about 150ml/5fl oz) of the simmering stock and stir continuously until the liquid has been absorbed, then add another ladleful and repeat the process. Keep adding the stock in this way until the rice is al dente – 16–18 minutes, then add a little more stock to loosen the risotto.

5. Mix all the ingredients for the lemon and basil mascarpone and serve a blob on top of each serving, with grated Parmesan.

Desserts

Baked creamy vanilla rice pudding

SERVES 4

Rice pudding is forever ingrained as one of the desserts of my childhood. Mum used to bake it rather than cook it on the hob so that it would come out with a golden topping but still be creamy underneath. I have tried using different jams in the bottom of the dish before the rice goes in and, perhaps unsurprisingly, I think raspberry works best. See page 176 for my simple jam recipe.

2 tbsp raspberry jam (optional)
75g (3oz) pearl rice/pudding rice
50g (2oz) caster sugar
700ml (1¼ pints) milk
150ml (5fl oz) regular or double cream
1 tsp vanilla extract

To serve
Roasted Rhubarb (see page 193)

1. Preheat the oven to 170°C (325°F), Gas mark 3.

2. If you want to add jam, spread it on the base of a 1 litre (1¾ pint) pie dish. Mix the rice and sugar together in a bowl and spread evenly over the bottom of the dish.

3. Pour the milk and cream into a large saucepan and bring to the boil. Stir in the vanilla extract, then carefully pour over the rice and sugar (I usually do this while the dish is sitting on the rack in the oven).

4. Bake in the oven for 1¼–1½ hours until the rice is soft and the top is golden.

5. Serve with roasted rhubarb and all its delicious juices.

Semolina with raspberry jam

SERVES 4–5

This is probably the dish I remember most from when I was very young. Still now I find a bowlful of this rib-sticking pudding the most comforting food of all. It's utterly delicious on its own, but I've also included a recipe for raspberry jam which makes the perfect accompaniment. Many people will tip the cooked, sweetened semolina into a buttered pie dish and bake it in an oven at 200°C (400°F), Gas mark 6 for about 20 minutes until golden on top – but we never did this at home, so I don't do it now.

1–2 tbsp sugar, to taste
500ml (18fl oz) milk
50g (2oz) fine semolina

For extra flavour
1 tsp vanilla extract
1 tsp finely grated lemon
 zest
½ tsp ground cinnamon
pinch of grated nutmeg or
 ground cardamom

For the raspberry jam
1kg (2lb 3oz) fresh or
 frozen raspberries
750g (1lb 10oz) granulated
 or caster sugar

1. Preheat the oven to 150°C (300°F), Gas mark 2. Place the sugar in an ovenproof bowl and put in the oven for 15 minutes to warm through.

2. Meanwhile, start making the jam. Place the raspberries in a large, wide saucepan set over a medium heat. Cook for a minute or two (or slightly longer if the fruit is frozen) until the fruit starts to break down and is juicy. Turn up the heat, bring to the boil and add the sugar to the raspberries. Stir until the sugar has dissolved, then boil for another 5–6 minutes, stirring frequently. If there is any scum on top (a pale pink froth, from dust or impurities in the fruit), skim it off with a slotted spoon and discard. Remove the pan from the heat while you test the jam to see if it is set (see tips, page 254). If the jam hasn't set, boil for a minute or so longer and test again. Once cooked, pour into sterilised jars (see tips page 254) and cover with lids or jam covers while still hot.

3. To make the semolina, place the milk in a saucepan and bring up to a simmer. Add the semolina and, using a whisk, stir it together to bring back to a simmer. Turn the heat down to low and continue to simmer and stir (using a whisk if you wish) for 7–8 minutes until the mixture has thickened. Sweeten to taste with sugar and add your chosen extra flavouring, if using.

4. Spoon out the semolina into individual bowls and top each with a dollop of jam and let everyone swirl it through the semolina themselves.

Rhubarb Eve's pudding

SERVES 6

A lovely old-fashioned British pudding that is normally made with apples. I love to experiment with other fruit sitting under the delicious buttery sponge, and the pretty pink delicious rhubarb works a treat. Serve with whipped cream or custard.

700g (1lb 9oz) rhubarb,
   sliced 5mm (¼in) thick
225g (8oz) sugar

For the sponge topping
110g (4oz) butter
110g (4oz) sugar
2 eggs
150g (5oz) plain flour
1 tsp baking powder
2 tsp vanilla extract
1 tbsp milk

To serve
a sprinkling of caster sugar
softly whipped cream or
   custard

1. Preheat oven to 180°C (350°F), Gas mark 4.

2. Place the rhubarb in a saucepan with the sugar and stir over a gentle heat to help the sugar to dissolve. Allow to bubble and boil, uncovered, until the rhubarb has softened and the mixture has thickened slightly, this will take 10–15 minutes. Pour into a 1 litre (1¾ pint) pie dish and set aside.

3. Next, prepare the sponge topping. In a bowl, cream the butter then beat in the sugar until light and fluffy. Beat in the eggs one at a time, then sift in the flour and the baking powder, stirring to mix. Lastly stir in the vanilla and the milk, then spoon over all the rhubarb to cover.

4. Bake in the oven for 30–35 minutes until the sponge is golden and feels set in the centre. Sprinkle some caster sugar over the top. Serve warm or at room temperature with softly whipped cream or custard.

Walnut tart

SERVES 6–8

A slice of this divine tart is a truly luxurious way to end a meal. This is wonderfully rich and nutty, topped with a simple icing made of sugar and Armagnac. Thanks to Jasper and his mum Julia for sharing this recipe with me. You can use regular brandy for this if you prefer.

For the pastry
225g (8oz) plain flour
1 tbsp caster sugar
pinch of sea salt
110g (4oz) butter, chilled
    and diced
2 egg yolks, beaten with
    2 tbsp water

For the filling
350g (12oz) crème fraîche
1 tsp vanilla extract
75g (3oz) caster sugar
175g (6oz) walnuts,
    chopped
2 egg whites
pinch of sea salt

1. First make the pastry. Place the flour, sugar and salt in a mixing bowl and rub in the butter until it resembles coarse breadcrumbs. Add half the beaten egg and water mixture and, using your hands, bring the pastry together. If it is dry, add a little more egg until it comes together. Do not knead it but shape it into a round, 2cm (¾in) thick, using your hands to flatten it. Cover with cling film and place in the fridge for 30 minutes (or up to 24 hours, or freeze for up to three months).

2. Alternatively, if you are making it in a food processor, whiz together the flour, sugar, salt and butter for a few seconds, then add half the beaten egg yolk and water mixture. Whiz for just a few seconds until it comes together – you might need to add a little more egg. Whichever method you use, hang on to any egg and water mix for brushing over the pastry when baking blind.

3. Preheat the oven to 180°C (350°F), Gas mark 4.

4. Take the pastry out of the fridge and place between two sheets of cling film. Roll it out until it is 3mm (⅛in) thick and large enough to line the base and sides of a 23cm (9in) tart tin. Remove the top layer of cling film, place the pastry upside down (cling film side facing up) into the tart tin (no need to flour or grease the tin). Press the pastry into the edges, cling film still attached, and, using your thumb 'cut' the pastry on the edge of the tin. If there are any holes or gaps, patch them with spare pastry. Remove the cling film and chill for 15 minutes.

5. Line the pastry with baking parchment (leaving plenty to come up the sides), fill with baking beans or dried pulses and bake for 20–25 minutes until the pastry feels just dry to the touch on the base. Remove the paper and beans, brush the pastry with leftover egg and water mix and return to the oven for 3 minutes. Patch any gaps with leftover raw pastry, as the filling will leak out of these otherwise. Once the pastry is baked blind take out of the oven, set aside in the tin while you make the filling. Set aside to cool and turn the oven up to 190°C (375°F), Gas mark 5.

For the icing
175g (6oz) icing sugar, plus
extra if needed
about 50ml (2fl oz)
Armagnac

To decorate
12 walnut halves

6. Next make the filling. Place the crème fraîche, vanilla and sugar in a bowl and whisk to combine. Mix in the walnuts. Next, place the egg whites and the pinch of salt in a clean, dry bowl and whisk until stiff. Fold into the walnut mixture then pour into the cooled pastry shell. Bake in the oven for 30 minutes until just set in the centre. Remove from the oven and leave to cool for 10 minutes before icing the tart. If you ice the tart while it's very hot, the icing will melt and sink down into the tart.

7. Before icing the tart, place the tart on a small bowl so that the sides of the tin fall down (make sure it's not catching anywhere that will prevent it from loosening easily) and place the tart on a flat serving plate. Remove, if you wish, the base of the tin by sliding a palette knife all round the bottom of the tart to free the pastry from the tin base, then carefully slide the base out to remove it.

8. To make the icing, sift the icing sugar into a bowl and add just enough Armagnac to make an icing that is easily spreadable. Add more icing sugar or Armagnac if it's too thin or thick. Very carefully ice the top of the tart (as the surface of the tart can easily tear). I normally do this by drizzling the icing all over the top of the tart, and before it has a chance to set I spread it using a palette knife that I regularly dip into boiling water. Once the tart is covered in the icing, decorate the tart by placing the walnut halves around the sides. Or you could coarsley chop the walnut halves and scatter them over the top. Set aside to let the icing dry then cut into slices to serve.

Apricot and cardamom bread and butter pudding

SERVES 4

I blame my Nordic roots for my obsession with cardamom. It works its magic with apricots in this divine and creamy bread-and-butter pudding recipe. Be sure to seek out plump green cardamom pods with aromatic black seeds inside.

10 fat green cardamom
   pods, peeled and crushed
   to give ¾ tsp
350ml (12fl oz) regular or
   double cream
150ml (5fl oz) milk
100g (3½oz) sugar (caster or
   granulated), plus 1 tbsp
3 eggs, beaten
1 tsp vanilla extract
50g (2oz) dried apricots,
   chopped
50ml (2fl oz) boiling water
6 slices of white bread,
   crusts removed (slightly
   stale if possible)
30g (1¼oz) soft butter

To serve
softly whipped cream

1. Place the crushed cardamom seeds in a saucepan with the cream, milk and the 100g (3½oz) of sugar. Stir over a high heat as it comes up to the boil and make sure the sugar dissolves. Once it comes to boiling point, turn off the heat and set aside for 2 minutes, then pour it onto the beaten eggs and vanilla extract, whisking all the time.

2. Next, place the chopped apricots in a cup or heatproof bowl and pour the boiling water over them. Set the apricots aside to plump up while you butter the bread.

3. Lay the bread out on your worktop and butter it with the soft butter. Cut the slices into 12 triangles. Lay 6 triangles of bread in the bottom of a 1 litre (1¾ pint) pie dish, buttered side up, then scatter the plumped apricots over the bread. Arrange the remaining triangles in a chevron design over the apricots. Add the cream and egg mixture, then sprinkle with the 1 tablespoon sugar and set aside for 1 hour if possible (or overnight).

4. Preheat the oven to 180°C (350°F), Gas mark 4 and place a bain marie of steaming water in the middle of the oven (a roasting tin half full with boiling water). Place the pie dish in the roasting tin and cook for 1 hour or until golden and puffed. Allow to cool slightly, then serve with softly whipped cream.

Lemon meringue pie

SERVES 4–6

A classic lemon meringue pie can be a joy to eat. Zingy lemon curd sitting inside
a buttery, crumbly pastry case, all covered with a blanket of fluffy white meringue.
Here's another gem from Jasper, courtesy of his mum, Julia.

For the pastry
225g (8oz) plain flour
½ tbsp caster sugar
170g (6oz) butter, chilled
    and diced
1 egg yolk, beaten with
    2 tbsp water

For the lemon curd
110g (4oz) butter
170g (6oz) caster sugar
finely grated zest and juice
    of 2 lemons
3 eggs, beaten

For the meringue
3 egg whites
150g (5oz) caster sugar

1. First make the pastry. Place the flour and the sugar in a mixing bowl and
   rub in the butter until it resembles coarse breadcrumbs. If the butter is really
   cold, you can grate it in for easier rubbing in.

2. Add half the beaten egg yolk and water and, using your hands, bring the
   pastry together. If it is too dry to come together, add a little more until it does.
   Do not knead it, but shape it into a round, 2cm (1in) thick, using your hands
   to flatten it. Cover with cling film and place in the fridge for 30 minutes or
   up to 24 hours (it can also be frozen for up to three months).

3. Alternatively, if you are making the pastry in a food processor, blitz the flour,
   sugar and the butter cubes. Whiz for a few seconds, then add half the beaten
   egg yolk and water and continue whizzing for just a second or two until it
   starts to come together. You might need to add a little more egg, but don't
   add too much, and don't overprocess the pastry otherwise it will be tough
   and heavy.

4. If you have any egg yolk and water left over, reserve it for brushing over
   the pastry at the end of the blind baking. Preheat the oven to 180°C (350°F),
   Gas mark 4.

5. You will need a 23cm (9in) metal tart tin with removable sides. Take the
   pastry out of the fridge and place between 2 sheets (larger than your tart tin)
   of cling film. Using a rolling pin, roll it out until it is 3mm (⅛in) thick. Make
   sure to keep it round, if the tin is round, and large enough to line the base
   and sides of the tin.

6. Removing just the top layer of cling film, place the pastry upside down (cling
   film side facing up) into the tart tin (no need to flour or grease the tin). Press
   the pastry into the edges, cling film still attached and, using your thumb, 'cut'
   the pastry on the edge of the tin. It should look quite neat. If there are any
   holes or gaps, patch them with some spare pastry. Remove the cling film
   and chill the pastry in the fridge for 15 minutes or even in the freezer for
   5 minutes (it will keep for weeks in the freezer, if covered well).

7. Bake blind by lining the pastry with baking parchment when chilled (leaving plenty of paper to come up the sides), fill with baking beans or dried pulses and bake for 20–25 minutes in the oven until the pastry feels just dry to the touch on the base. Remove the paper and beans, brush with a little leftover beaten egg yolk and water (or a bit of new beaten egg if there's none of the yolk and water left over) and return to the oven for 3 minutes. Again, if there are any little holes or cracks in the pastry, just patch it up with any leftover raw pastry as the filling will leak out of these in the oven if not patched up. Once the pastry is baked blind, take out of the oven and set the pastry aside in the tin to cool. This can be easily made a day in advance and covered until you need it. Leave the oven on at the same temperature.

8. To make the lemon curd, over a very low heat melt the butter with the sugar, lemon zest and the juice (that you've poured through a sieve). Add the beaten eggs and stir carefully over a low heat until the mixture has thickened and will coat the back of a spoon, holding the mark that your finger makes when your draw a line through it. Take off the heat and pour into a bowl to cool. Place the cooled lemon curd into the cooled pastry shell and set aside.

9. Next, make the meringue. Place the egg whites in a clean, dry bowl and, using an electric whisk, beat them until they start to hold stiff peaks. Next add 1 tablespoon of the sugar and continue to whisk until stiff, then fold in the remaining sugar. Spread the meringue over the lemon curd to fill the tart tin, using the back of a spoon to lift up little snowy meringue peaks all over the top.

10. Place the pie in the oven and bake for 10 minutes until deep golden on top. Remove from the oven and leave to stand for 5 minutes before removing carefully from the tin and transferring to a serving plate. Cut into slices to serve.

Cullohill apple pie – Darina's mum's apple pie

SERVES 8–10

Darina's late mother, Elizabeth O'Connell, could make pastry and bread like no other. And bringing up nine children as well as serving food in her pub, The Sportman's Inn in Cullohill, Co. Laois, she sure had a lot of practice. This is the pie that she baked every single day for the pub. It's also great with other fruit such as rhubarb, plums or gooseberries.

700g (1lb 9oz) cooking apples
150g (5oz) caster sugar, plus extra for sprinkling
3 cloves
1 egg, beaten
a very small splash of milk

For the pastry
225g (8oz) butter
50g (2oz) caster sugar
2 eggs
350g (12oz) plain flour, plus extra for dusting

1. First, make the pastry. Cream the butter and sugar together by hand or in a food mixer. Add the eggs, one by one, then reduce the speed and mix in the flour. Turn out onto a piece of floured baking parchment and flatten into a round, then wrap and chill for 1 hour, or overnight, if possible.

2. Preheat the oven to 180°C (350°F), Gas mark 4. Roll out the pastry on a lightly floured surface to a thickness of 3mm (⅛in). Use a little less than two-thirds of the pastry to line a 18 x 32 x 2.5cm (7 x 12½ x 1in) tin or a 23cm (9in) diameter round tin. Roll the remaining third to a rectangle or circle to fit the tin as a lid.

3. Peel, core and dice the apples into 2cm (¾in) chunks and place in the tin. Sprinkle with sugar and add the cloves. Brush a little water around the pastry rim and lay the pastry lid over the apples, pressing the pastry edges together to seal. Use the leftover pastry to make shapes to decorate the top. Combine the beaten egg and milk to make an eggwash and brush over the pastry.

4. Bake in the oven for 45–60 minutes until the apples are tender and the pastry is a rich golden brown. Sprinkle with sugar to serve.

Elizabeth, Darina's mother.

Rose and saffron panna cotta

Rose water can vary hugely in strength, so do taste this and add more if it needs it.
Adding a few pomegranate seeds to the strawberries will be lovely, too.

300ml (½ pint) regular or
    double cream
25g (1oz) caster sugar
pinch of saffron strands
1 leaf of gelatine
¼ tsp rose water, or to taste
sunflower oil (optional – see
    tip)

To serve
strawberries, quartered,
    and tossed with a little
    sugar if necessary

1. Put the cream, sugar and saffron in a saucepan and slowly bring up to a simmer. Turn off the heat and set aside.

2. Meanwhile, put the gelatine leaf into a bowl with enough water to cover it. After 4–5 minutes it will have softened completely. At that point, take it out of the water and put into the saucepan with the hot cream. Whisk gently until the gelatine dissolves. If the cream has cooled down too much you might need to reheat it slightly with the gelatine. Add the rose water and taste to see if you need a bit more.

3. Pour into oiled ramekins (if you want to turn them out, see tips), pretty glasses, little cups or whatever you fancy. Leave for 3 hours in the fridge to set.

4. Serve with some gorgeous, sweet strawberries.

TIPS
Panna cotta should be quite soft and wobbly in consistency, but if you like you can turn it out. Just oil the ramekin with a little sunflower oil before you put in the mixture.

Panna cotta is normally made with 100 per cent cream, but if you want a slightly lighter panna cotta, use half milk, half cream or three-quarters cream and one-quarter milk.

You can use powdered gelatine instead of leaf – just follow the instructions on the box; 1 leaf = 1 rounded tsp.

Mother's plum shortcake

SERVES 6

This recipe comes from my friend Helen's mother's mother's mother (her great-grandmother). She was, however, always known as 'mother'. To their knowledge the recipe is over 150 years old and has been passed on from generation to generation. Helen has huge memories of it from her childhood – either from Sunday lunches or Saturday mornings from the dinner party leftovers – the smell takes her right back to feeling small again! Her mother recalls that her grandmother, Nan Nan in New Zealand, was in fierce competition with her two eldest sisters throughout their long lives to make the best shortcake.

For the shortcake
225g (8oz) plain flour
225g (8oz) caster sugar
2 tsp baking powder
1 tsp ground cinnamon
110g (4oz) butter
2 eggs, beaten (you may not need it all)
a little milk, if needed
icing sugar, for dusting (optional)

For the stewed plums
8 ripe plums, pitted and each half cut in quarters
110g (4oz) sugar

To serve
softly whipped cream or vanilla ice cream

1. First make the shortcake dough. Place the flour, caster sugar, baking powder and cinnamon in a bowl, then rub in the butter. Add nearly all the egg and bring together with your hands, using the last of the egg if you need it. Pat the dough out so that it's 1cm (½in) thick and cover with cling film or baking parchment or pop into a plastic bag, then put into the fridge for at least 30 minutes.

2. Place the plums in a pan with the sugar over a medium-low heat. Using a wooden spoon, slightly bash the plums so that they lose some of the juices and create a syrup in which they will cook. Cover and cook over a low heat for 20 minutes or until completely tender and broken up. Take the lid off after 10 minutes so that the juice evaporates. Take off the heat and allow to cool.

3. Preheat the oven to 180°C (350°F), Gas mark 4 and butter a small Swiss roll tin.

4. Roll out half the dough on a floured surface into a rectangle almost as large as the tin, but not quite. It will puff up and spread, so it doesn't need to fill the tin exactly and it will be quite soft, but don't worry. Lift the dough on to the buttered tray, cover with the cooled stewed fruit and top with another layer of rolled-out pastry, closing the ends together. Brush the top with any remaining egg (you can add a small splash of milk to the egg to make it go further).

5. Bake on a lower shelf in the oven for 40 minutes until golden brown all over and a skewer comes out clean when inserted into the centre.

6. Dust with icing sugar, if you like. Serve hot or cold – for dessert or afternoon tea – with softly whipped cream or vanilla ice cream.

TIP
Helen's great-grandmother used to make this with apples, but so many other fruits work well in this, too. I love using plums.

Mum celebrating Christmas with her younger sister, Kristin (above), as well as my great-grandmother, Clara (below).

Icelandic crêpes with roasted rhubarb and sweet vanilla cream

SERVES 4–6, MAKES 8–12 CRÊPES

An Icelandic classic, this is a sweet treat I never tire of.
Sometimes I add sliced strawberries to the roasted rhubarb, too.

For the crêpe batter
175g (6oz) plain flour
1 tbsp caster sugar
pinch of salt
3 eggs
225ml (8fl oz) milk
25g (1oz) butter, for
 greasing the pan

For the sweet vanilla cream
250ml (9fl oz) double or
 regular cream
1 tbsp icing sugar
1 tsp vanilla extract or the
 seeds scraped from
 ¼ vanilla pod

For the roasted rhubarb
300g (11oz) rhubarb
50g (2oz) butter
100g (3½oz) caster sugar

1. First, make the crêpe batter. Sift the flour into a bowl and mix in the sugar and salt. Make a well in the centre and drop in the eggs. Pour the milk into a jug and add 225ml (8fl oz) water. Pour onto the eggs, whisking all the time from the centre, gradually drawing in the flour from the sides of the bowl. Whisk well until the mixture is combined to create a smooth batter. You can set the batter aside if you wish – it will store in the fridge for up to two days, or cook it straight away.

2. When you're ready to cook the crêpes, place a frying pan over a high heat and allow to get hot. Pour the batter into a jug and give it a quick whisk to mix it. Fold up a piece or two of kitchen paper and have next to you a warm plate for the cooked crêpes and a fish slice or palette knife to lift them with.

3. When the pan is nice and hot, place a small knob of butter in the pan and immediately, before it has a chance to burn, wipe it around with the kitchen paper. Make sure the whole base of the pan has been buttered. Straight away pour in a little batter and quickly swirl the pan so that the batter covers it, making sure it's not too thick. If there are gaps, pour in a drizzle to patch it. Once light golden underneath, turn the crêpe with the fish slice or palette knife and cook the other side.

4. Transfer the crêpe to the warm plate and repeat with the remaining batter until all the crêpes are cooked, laying them on top of each other. After every one or two crêpes, grease the pan again with the buttered kitchen paper.

5. Next, make the sweet vanilla cream. Whip the cream in a bowl with the icing sugar and vanilla until soft peaks form. Keep in the fridge until needed.

6. To roast the rhubarb, preheat the oven to 230ºC (450ºF), Gas mark 8. Slice the rhubarb at an angle into pieces 3cm (1¼in) long, then tip into a bowl. Place the butter and sugar in a saucepan and stir to melt the butter. Pour over the rhubarb and stir to mix, then spread out in a single layer in a baking tray. Roast in the oven for 12 minutes or until tender and a little scorched around the edges.

7. To serve, place two or three crêpes on each plate and fold each in quarters. Spoon the warm rhubarb and sauce over, top with sweet vanilla cream and serve.

Stewed plums with saffron crème anglaise

When I asked my friend Fingal Ferguson of Gubbeen Smokehouse what recipes of his Mum's did he love as a child, one of the first that he mentioned was stewed plums with crème anglaise. The addition of saffron to my crème anglaise here is a nod to the fabulous Giana, Fingal's mum, and her Spanish upbringing.

350g (12oz) caster or granulated sugar
1 vanilla pod, halved lengthways
9 ripe plums, halved and pitted

For the saffron crème anglaise
500ml (18fl oz) milk
1 pinch of saffron strands
5 egg yolks
100g (3½oz) caster sugar

1. First prepare the plums. Place the sugar, 350ml (12fl oz) water and the vanilla pod in a saucepan over a medium heat, bring to the boil and boil for 2 minutes.

2. Put the plums into the hot syrup. Bring back to the boil and cook over a medium heat for 15–20 minutes until completely softened. Take off the heat and allow to cool slightly before serving. If you want to eat them later, they will store perfectly in the fridge for a couple of weeks.

3. While the plums cool, make the crème anglaise. Pour the milk into a large saucepan and add the saffron. Place over a medium-low heat and slowly bring to the boil.

4. Meanwhile, beat the egg yolks and sugar together in a large heatproof bowl until pale and thick. Gradually whisk the hot milk into the beaten eggs and sugar, and pour the whole mixture back into the saucepan.

5. Return to a low heat and cook very gently for 5–8 minutes, stirring all the time, until the custard thickens slightly (it should just coat the back of the spoon).

6. Pour the saffron crème anglaise into a warm jug. Reheat the plums, if you like, and serve with the crème anglaise.

Plum crumble

SERVES 4–6

Using leftover bread to make breadcrumbs instead of using flour for a crumble topping has a long history, and Pam, one of the great teachers at the cookery school, remembers her mum Sheila doing this when Pam was young. The crumbs soak up the butter beautifully, bringing a deliciously rich crunch on top of the fruit.

For the stewed plums
6 large plums, halved, pitted and each half cut into 1cm (½in) chunks
125g (4½oz) soft light brown sugar

For the breadcrumb crumble
100g (3½oz) fresh breadcrumbs
100g (3½oz) Demerara, light muscovado or soft light brown sugar
½ tsp ground cinnamon (optional)
75g (3oz) butter

To serve
softly whipped cream or vanilla ice cream

1. First make the stewed plums. Place the plums in a saucepan with the sugar and 50ml (2fl oz) water over a medium-high heat. Stir as the mixture heats up to dissolve the sugar, then cover the pan with a lid and cook over a medium-low heat for 5–10 minutes until the plums have just softened. Remove the lid and cook the plums for another 5–10 minutes until the mixture has thickened slightly and the plums are completely tender.

2. Tip the plums and all their sweet juices into a shallow 1 litre (1¾ pint) pie dish or 4 or 6 individual ovenproof dishes.

3. Next, make the crumble. Place the breadcrumbs, sugar and ground cinnamon (if using) in a mixing bowl. Cut the butter into small cubes and rub into the breadcrumb mixture, just until slightly coarse.

4. Tip the crumble mixture over the fruit and bake in the preheated oven for 20–25 minutes until the fruit is bubbling up around the edges and the crumble is golden. It will get deliciously crunchy as it cools slightly.

5. Serve warm with softly whipped cream or vanilla ice cream.

Mum's syllabub with shortbread fingers

SERVES 4

A classic syllabub is a light, creamy Victorian pudding often enjoyed with crumbly shortbread biscuits. This is a slightly different version, but still with the fluffy texture and sweet flavour from the redcurrant jelly.

250ml (9fl oz) regular or
    double cream
125ml (4½fl oz) white wine
50g (2oz) caster sugar
finely grated zest of
    1 orange
2 egg whites
1 tbsp redcurrant jelly

For the shortbread fingers
150g (5oz) plain flour
50g (2oz) caster sugar, plus
    extra to dust
100g (3½oz) butter, softened

1. First make the shortbread fingers. Preheat the oven to 180°C (350°F), Gas mark 4. Place the flour in a bowl with the sugar and mix together, then rub in the butter and squeeze the mixture in your hands to bring it together to form a dough. Alternatively, you could bring the ingredients together very briefly in a food processor using the blade.

2. Roll out the dough out until 5mm (¼in) thick, keeping it in a square or a rectangle. Pierce it all over with a skewer or fork, then cut it into fingers 10 x 2cm (4 x ¾in) in size. Place on a baking sheet (no need to grease or line) and bake for 5–8 minutes until light golden. Take out and leave to stand for 2 minutes before transferring to a cooling rack.

3. While the shortbread cools, make the syllabub. Place the cream in a bowl with the wine and sugar and whisk until fluffy. Fold in most of the orange zest but leave a little aside for scattering over the top when serving. Spoon into four individual glasses or a bowl.

4. Next, place the egg whites and redcurrant jelly in a clean, dry bowl and whisk together until the mixture is holding stiff peaks. Spoon this over the wine and cream mixture, then scatter with the remaining zest.

5. Place in the fridge until you're ready to serve. Dust the shortbread fingers with caster sugar and serve alongside the syllabub.

Three-seed pumpernickel

MAKES 1 X 900G (2LB) LOAF

At an event I was working at recently, I got talking to a lovely young Icelandic mother who is now based in Ireland. Lara Jonasdottir ('daughter of Jonas'), who is a herbalist and reflexologist in Galway, has shared with me many of her mother's and grandmother's Icelandic recipes. This delicious bread recipe is inspired by a traditional Laugarvatn (where Lara's great-grandmother lived) hot-spring rye bread, *hverbrauð*, which is baked in the hot ground for about 24 hours before being served hot or at room temperature with butter and *síld* – pickled herrings. *Takk*, Lara!

1 tbsp sunflower oil, plus extra for greasing
300g (11oz) rye flour
150g (5oz) wholemeal flour
50g (2oz) bulgur wheat
30g (1¼oz) sunflower seeds
30g (1¼oz) pumpkin seeds
1 tsp caraway seeds
1 tsp salt
2 tbsp treacle (60g/2½oz)

1. Line a 900g (2lb) loaf tin with baking parchment.

2. Mix all the dry ingredients together in a bowl. Put the treacle in a bowl or jug, add 400ml (14fl oz) warm water and the oil and stir well to dissolve the treacle. Make a well in the centre of the flour and seeds mixture and add the liquids, then mix well to form a sticky dough. Transfer to the prepared tin and smooth the top, then cover with foil and allow to stand overnight or for up to 48 hours.

3. Next day, preheat the oven to 110°C (225°F), Gas mark ¼. Place the loaf, still covered with the foil, in the oven and cook for 6 hours.

4. Remove the foil and turn the loaf out of the tin. Put back in the oven and cook for a further 2 hours. Transfer to a wire rack to cool.

Rye and sesame bread

MAKES 1 X 900G (2LB) LOAF

When talking to Lara about her favourite food from Iceland, rye bread was mentioned a lot, going with everything from smoked fish and gravlax to sliced meats and cheese. This bread recipe is a variation of the original Ballymaloe brown yeast bread, which is itself based on a no-knead wholemeal yeast loaf famously created by a baker named Doris Grant during the Second World War.

1 generous tsp treacle or molasses
25g (1oz) fresh yeast or 12g (½oz) dried yeast
150g (5oz) wholemeal rye flour
150g (5oz) wholemeal bread flour
100g (3½oz) strong white flour
25g (1oz) sesame seeds
1 tsp sea salt
sunflower oil and 1–2 tbsp sesame seeds, to prepare the tin

1. Stir the treacle or molasses into 450ml (16fl oz) warm water and then crumble in the yeast, but don't stir it in. Leave to stand for 5 minutes or until the yeast starts to froth.

2. While you're waiting, place the rye flour, the wholemeal flour and the strong white flour in a large mixing bowl. Add the sesame seeds and the salt and mix to combine. Check the yeast mixture – the surface will look a bit fizzy or frothy when it's ready.

3. Make a well in the centre of the dry ingredients, stir the yeast mixture well and pour all but 50ml (2fl oz) of the liquid into the dry ingredients. Mix well to bring together – it should be soft and sloppy. If it's not, add the remaining water. Allow the mixture to stand in the mixing bowl for 5 minutes.

4. While the mixture is standing, brush the inside of a 900g (2lb) loaf tin with sunflower oil and shake some sesame seeds in the base and on the sides of the tin. Pour the wet dough into the tin, levelling the top, then scatter with some sesame seeds if you wish. Lay a clean, dry tea towel over the top and leave to rise in a warm part of your kitchen for 15–25 minutes until almost doubled in size.

5. Preheat an oven to 220°C (425°F), Gas mark 7.

6. When the dough has risen, carefully place it in the centre of the preheated oven and cook it for 1 hour, turning the oven down to 200°C (400°F), Gas mark 6 after 15 minutes. Five minutes before it's ready, take the bread out of the oven, tip it out of the tin and place the loaf back into the oven for 5 minutes to crisp up the sides. When the bread is cooked, take it out of the oven and allow to cool.

Sue's oatmeal bread

MAKES 1 X 900G (2LB) LOAF

This recipe surprised me from the start. When Sue Cullinane, one of our great teachers at Ballymaloe, told me about this simple bread from her childhood made from oats, yoghurt and a couple of other ingredients, I was not so sure. I was even less sure the first time I tried making it myself, as I tipped the heavy, dense dough into the tin. But hey presto, after 1 hour in the oven I realised I had a gorgeously nutty and nutritious loaf, not dissimilar to a great brown soda bread.

425g (15oz) rolled oats (not jumbo or pinhead)
¾ tsp sea salt
2 tsp bread soda (bicarbonate of soda)
2 tbsp mixed seeds
1 egg
500g (1lb 2oz) natural yoghurt

1. Preheat the oven to 200°C (400°F), Gas mark 6. Line the base of a 900g (2lb) loaf tin with baking parchment.

2. In a large bowl, mix the oats, salt, bread soda and mixed seeds.

3. Whisk the egg into the yoghurt. Pour the yoghurt and eggs into the dry ingredients and mix well. The dough is meant to be dry and sticky at this stage so don't worry.

4. Scoop the dough into the tin and bake for 50 minutes.

5. Turn out of the loaf tin and bake for a further 10 minutes. Allow to cool on a wire rack.

TIP
If you use a 500g (1lb 2oz) pot of yoghurt, you can measure the oats by filling the pot twice.

White soda focaccia with shallots, walnuts and blue cheese

SERVES 8–12

The love child of an Italian focaccia and an Irish soda bread, this is a quick and nifty bread that can be topped with countless other delicious ingredients. Just don't scrimp on the extra-virgin olive oil!

For the dough
extra-virgin olive oil, for greasing
450g (1lb) plain flour, plus extra for dusting
½ tsp salt
½ tsp bread soda (bicarbonate of soda)
400ml (14fl oz) buttermilk

For the topping
4 shallots, peeled, sliced through the root and cut into 8 wedges
125g (4½oz) blue cheese, broken into odd chunks
10 walnuts, broken into pieces
2 tbsp extra-virgin olive oil
good pinch of sea salt flakes

1. Preheat the oven to 210°C (400°F), Gas mark 7. Oil a 23 x 33cm (9 x 13in) Swiss roll tin with 1 tablespoon olive oil.

2. First prepare the topping. Mix the shallots, blue cheese and walnuts with the oil in a bowl and set aside.

3. Next start on the bread. In a large bowl, mix all the dry ingredients for the dough. Make a well in the centre, then pour in nearly all the buttermilk, leaving 25ml (1fl oz). With your hand, mix the milk into the flour to form a soft dough that isn't too sticky or too dry. Add the remaining milk if necessary (the consistency of buttermilk can vary, the thicker it is the more you will need). Turn the dough out onto a floured work surface and roll it over once or twice to form an even ball that is lightly dusted with flour, but do not knead the dough or it will become tough and heavy.

4. Transfer the dough to the prepared tin and, with floury fingers, push the dough out evenly to the edges and corners of the tin. Then, poke little dents into the top of the dough for the oil to spill into and generously drizzle with more olive oil.

5. Scatter the cheese, shallot and walnut mixture evenly over the dough and sprinkle with salt flakes, then bake in the oven for 30–40 minutes.

6. Take out of the oven and transfer to a wire rack to cool. Serve while it is still warm.

Buttermilk burger buns

The buttermilk in these buns really helps to develop a lovely soft, tender crumb.
Make a big batch while you're at it, and freeze the cooked split buns for convenience.

600g (1lb 5oz) strong white
   flour, plus extra for
   dusting
1 tsp sea salt
50g (2oz) butter
1 tbsp sugar
350ml (12fl oz) buttermilk
20g (¾oz) fresh yeast or
   10g (½oz) dried yeast
1 egg, beaten, plus a little
   extra beaten egg for
   brushing
sesame seeds, for scattering

1. Preheat the oven to 220°C (425°F), Gas mark 7. Liberally coat two baking sheets with flour and set aside.

2. Sift the flour into a large bowl and mix in the salt.

3. Melt the butter in a pot, add the sugar and then the buttermilk and warm up to 37°C (98°F) on a thermometer – tepid to the touch. No hotter than this or you will kill the yeast. If it gets too hot, let it cool to the correct temperature.

4. Put the yeast in a bowl and add the beaten egg and warmed buttermilk mixture. Give it a little stir and leave to stand for a few minutes to allow the yeast to dissolve. Give it another little stir and then make a well in the flour and add the liquid. Bring it to a soft dough and knead it in a food mixer or by hand for at least 10 minutes. Press the dough with a floured finger – it should spring back nicely. Place the dough in a large bowl and cover with cling film. Place in a warm part of your kitchen and allow the dough to rise until light and doubled in size. It'll take 1–2 hours. Or you could put it into the fridge overnight.

5. Knock the dough back by punching and kneading it for 2 minutes. Divide into 10–12 even-sized balls, then shape into flat buns 10cm (4in) in diameter. Place, spaced well apart, on the baking sheets and leave to rise again.

6. When risen, brush each bun with a little beaten egg and sprinkle with sesame seeds. If baking in a fan oven, bake both sheets for 10–15 minutes, or one at a time in a conventional oven.

7. Take out of the oven and transfer to a wire rack, then cover with a tea towel and allow to cool.

8. Serve with a juicy burger and lot of tasty toppings.

Cheesy white soda swirls

Eaten warm, not long out of the oven, these are a joy to behold and are divine with a big bowl of warming soup and a good movie. The key to making a good soda bread is not to overhandle the dough. You don't want to knead this mixture, otherwise it will be tough.

110g (3¾oz) mature Cheddar cheese, grated
¼ tsp cayenne pepper
450g (1lb) plain flour, plus extra for dusting
½ tsp bread soda (bicarbonate of soda)
1 tsp sea salt
25g (1oz) butter, cut into cubes
375–400ml (13–14fl oz) buttermilk (if the buttermilk is very thick you may need more), plus extra for brushing

1. Preheat the oven to 220°C (425°F), Gas mark 7.

2. Mix the grated Cheddar with the cayenne pepper and set aside. Sift the flour and bicarbonate of soda into a bowl. Mix in the salt and then rub in the butter until it resembles coarse breadcrumbs. Make a well in the centre and add the buttermilk. Using your hand, stretched out like a claw and starting from the middle and going around the bowl in one direction, bring the mixture together, but make sure not to knead it.

3. Once it comes together, tip the dough out onto a floured worktop. Roll it out into a rectangle 40 x 15cm (15¾ x 6in), dusting with flour. It should be quite thin, 1cm (½in) thick. Dust the excess flour away from the top of the dough, then brush buttermilk all over and scatter with the grated cheese and cayenne pepper mix.

4. Starting at the long end, roll the dough so that it looks like a Swiss roll. Cut it into 12 slices, 2.5cm (1in) thick each, and place on a baking sheet (no need to flour or line the sheet).

5. Bake in the oven for 5 minutes, then lower the oven temperature to 200°C (400°F), Gas mark 6 and cook for a further 12–15 minutes until golden brown and hollow sounding when tapped on the bottom. Turn out and cool on a wire rack.

Charlotte's Swedish seed crackers

MAKES 2 TRAYS

The Swedes are famous for their crackers. I've enjoyed so many versions of Swedish *knäckebröd,* both here and in Scandinavia. This great recipe comes from the wonderful Charlotte Berner, a Swedish friend of ours whose son Ted is married to one of my many cousins-in-law. The psyllium husks are available in good health food shops. These are delicious just spread with butter or topped with cheese, smoked salmon or gravlax.

200g (7oz) sunflower seeds
130g (4½oz) pumpkin seeds
70g (2½oz) flaxseeds
70g (2½oz) sesame seeds
2 tbsp psyllium husks
2 tbsp almond flour,
    plus extra for dusting
    (optional)
1 tsp sea salt, plus extra for
    sprinkling
poppy seeds, for sprinkling

1. Preheat the oven to 170°C (325°F), Gas mark 3. Line two baking sheets with baking parchment.

2. In a large bowl, mix all the ingredients together with 450ml (16fl oz) water (it should be the consistency of watery porridge).

3. Divide in half and roll out as thinly as possible on the baking parchment, using more almond flour to stop the mixture sticking, if needed.

4. Sprinkle with sea salt and poppy seeds.

5. Bake in the oven for 70 minutes or until dry.

6. Store in pieces in an airtight tin. Keep dry and pop into a hot oven for a few minutes before serving to crisp them up if they've softened slightly.

Darina's mother, Elizabeth, doing some pruning (above), and with Darina (below).

Spotted soda loaf

One of the first breads that I was taught to make by my mother-in-law (eight years before she became my mother-in-law!) was a classic Irish recipe that has been handed down through the generations in every family. It was sweetened white soda bread dotted all over with raisins and sultanas. This is a slight variation of that bread with some added butter for a lovely soft, tender crumb.

25g (1oz) butter, plus extra
  for greasing
350g (12oz) plain flour, plus
  extra for dusting
scant ½ tsp bread soda
  (bicarbonate of soda)
1 tsp salt
100g (3½oz) sultanas
1 egg
250ml (9fl oz) buttermilk

1. Preheat the oven to 200°C (400°F), Gas mark 6. Brush a 450g (1lb) loaf tin generously with melted butter and then lightly dust with flour.

2. Rub the butter into the flour in a large bowl and then mix in the remaining dry ingredients including the sultanas.

3. Whisk the egg into the buttermilk. Make a well in the centre of the flour mix and pour in nearly all the buttermilk – leaving about 25ml (1fl oz). Mix to a soft dough and then add the remaining buttermilk if you need to (the consistency of buttermilk can vary, the thicker it is the more you will need).

4. Place the dough in the prepared loaf tin and bake for 50 minutes.

5. Turn out of the loaf tin and bake for a further 10–15 minutes to firm up the crust until crisp and a golden colour. Allow to cool on a wire rack.

Sweet scones

MAKES 8–10 SCONES

Another one of Darina's mum's recipes – these are the kind of scones that we make almost daily at the cookery school at Ballymaloe. Light and fluffy, they are completely divine with butter and jam – or for more of a special treat, with jam and cream. Feel free to add your favourite dried fruits, some grated orange zest or even chocolate chips to these scones, just stir them in with the flour and sugar at the start.

450g (1lb) plain flour, plus extra for dusting
pinch of sea salt
2 tsp baking powder
25g (1oz) caster sugar
75g (3oz) butter, softened
2 eggs
200ml (7fl oz) milk

For the crunchy glaze (optional but oh-so-good)
1 small egg, beaten (if there is no liquid left from the scones)
a few tbsp granulated sugar

To serve
butter, jam, whipped cream or clotted cream

1. First preheat the oven to 230°C/ 450°F/Gas mark 8.

2. Lightly flour a baking sheet. Sift the flour, salt and baking powder into a large bowl, add the sugar and mix. Rub in the butter and make a well in the centre. In another bowl, whisk the eggs with the milk. Pour all but 50ml (2 fl oz) of this liquid into the dry ingredients and using one hand, outstretched like a claw, going in large circles around the inside of the bowl, mix to a soft dough, adding more of the liquid, if necessary.

3. Turn out onto a floured work surface and gently turn it over to show what will probably be the smoother side. Be careful not to knead the mixture or the scones will be tough. Dust with flour and gently roll out until it is 2.5cm (1in) thick. Cut with a knife or into rounds using a 7cm (2¾in) cutter into scones.

4. If you opt for a crunchy glaze, put the granulated sugar in a shallow bowl or saucer. Brush the beaten egg over the tops of the scones, or use the remaining beaten eggs and milk, and dip, egg side down, into the sugar. Place the sugared scones on the prepared baking sheet, slightly spaced apart from each other, and bake in the centre of the preheated oven for 12–15 minutes, depending on their size, until a rich gold on top. They should feel light, and sound hollow when you tap them on their bases when baked. Cool on a wire rack, then split in two and spread with butter and jam, or jam and cream. These are completely divine when served still a little warm, fresh out of the oven.

Sweet white milk bun dough

MAKES 12 BUNS

This yeast-risen dough has a tender and soft crumb from the milk and butter it contains. It is perfect for sweet treats. It's also incredibly versatile – these are just a few variations.

150ml (5fl oz) milk
25g (1oz) fresh yeast or
   12.5g (½oz) dried yeast
450g (1lb) strong white
   flour
40g (1½oz) sugar
pinch of salt
75g (3oz) butter, diced
1 egg
sunflower oil, for greasing

1. Warm the milk until hand-hot – 37°C (98°F) – on a sugar thermometer. Crumble the yeast into a bowl, pour over the warm milk and set aside for 5 minutes.

2. Mix the flour with the sugar and salt, then rub in the butter cubes.

3. Next, whisk the egg into the milk and yeast, and slowly pour this mixture into the flour. Mix well to form a soft dough – it should not be too dry or too sticky at this stage – it should not stick to your hands but there should be no dry crumbs either. Knead it well, by hand or in a food mixer with a dough hook, if you wish, until you have a soft springy dough, 10 minutes.

4. Transfer to a lightly oiled bowl about three times larger than the ball of dough. Cover with cling film and leave to rise in a warm part of your kitchen for 1 hour or until almost doubled in size.

5. Remove from the bowl, knock it back with your fists lightly, then knead for 2 minutes. Once kneaded, shape as required.

Bun wash

Use as a glaze for the buns and for poaching fruit such as plums, rhubarb and apricots.

100g (3½oz) sugar
100ml (3½fl oz) water

1. Place the sugar and water in a saucepan and cook, stirring, over a medium heat until the sugar has dissolved.

2. Turn up the heat and boil the sugar solution, uncovered, for 2 minutes, then set aside until needed.

Jam and cream buns

MAKES 12 BUNS

There is something wonderfully comforting about an old-fashioned jam and cream bun.
Fresh out of the oven and filled with sweetened vanilla-scented cream and a great fruity
preserve, this is one of my favourites.

1 x Sweet White Milk Bun
   Dough (see opposite)
flour, for dusting
1 x Bun Wash (see opposite)
3–4 tbsp strawberry or
   raspberry jam (see page
   176 for my recipe)

**For the sweet Chantilly
cream**
150ml (5fl oz) regular or
   double cream
1–2 tbsp icing sugar, sifted,
   plus extra for dusting
½ tsp vanilla extract

1. Preheat the oven to 200°C/400°F/Gas mark 6.

2. Divide the dough into 12 balls. On a clean, unfloured work surface, roll each
   ball under the palm of your hand to form a round bun, working clockwise
   and anti-clockwise then rolling it up and down. Roll each bun into a thick
   sausage shape. Cover any dough that's waiting to be rolled with a tea towel.

3. Place the dough sausages on a lightly floured baking sheet, spaced apart from
   each other. Cover the sheet with a tea towel and leave the dough to rise in a
   warm part of your kitchen for 1 hour or until almost doubled in size. When
   you press the dough gently, they should feel airy and the dent of your finger
   should remain.

4. Bake in the oven for 15 minutes or until golden and cooked through. The
   buns should feel hollow when you tap them on the base. Take them out of
   the oven and brush them straight away with the bun wash, then allow to cool
   on a wire rack.

5. While the buns are cooling, make the Chantilly cream. Whip the cream
   to soft peaks, then fold in the icing sugar and vanilla extract until evenly
   combined.

6. When the buns are cool, split each one horizontally through the middle, but
   not right through, and spoon in or pipe a long line of jam, then a generous
   line of sweet Chantilly cream. Dust with icing sugar and serve!

Cinnamon bun cluster

MAKES 12 BUNS

The most indulgent of the buns, these are a no-holds-barred treat to have with, or without, a cup of coffee.

melted butter, for greasing
flour, for dusting
2 tsp ground cinnamon
1 x Sweet White Milk Bun
Dough (see page 216)

For the cinnamon butter
glaze
50g (2oz) butter
75g (3oz) caster sugar
1 tsp ground cinnamon

1. Preheat the oven to 200°C (400°F), Gas mark 6.

2. Brush the sides of a 25cm (10in) springform cake tin with melted butter and dust with flour, then shake out any excess flour.

3. Knead the cinnamon into the dough. Divide the dough into 12 balls and roll on a clean worktop under the palms of your hands to make round buns. Cover any dough that's waiting to be rolled with a tea towel. Place them slightly spaced apart in the tin, three in the centre and nine around the sides, making sure the neater sides are facing up. Cover with a tea towel and leave to rise in a warm part of your kitchen for 1 hour or until almost doubled in size. When you press the dough gently, they should feel airy and the dent of your finger should remain.

3. Place in the preheated oven for 35–40 minutes or until golden and cooked all the way through.

4. Meanwhile, make the glaze by boiling the butter, sugar, cinnamon and 50ml (2fl oz) water together for 2–3 minutes until slightly thickened, stirring continuously to dissolve the sugar before it boils.

5. Take the cluster out of the oven and leave to stand for 2 minutes before taking out of the tin and placing on a serving plate.

6. Immediately pour over the hot cinnamon butter glaze, using a pastry brush to help you cover every bit of the top of the cluster. Allow to cool a little, and then serve.

Iced cardamom buns

Cardamom is the spice of choice for many Scandinavian bakers and I love how it brings its intriguing sweetness to these delicious iced buns.

20 nice fat green cardamom pods, peeled and seeds crushed (see tip)
1 x Sweet White Milk Bun Dough (see page 216)
1 x Bun Wash (see page 216)

For the icing
juice of ¼–½ lemon
175g (6oz) icing sugar, sifted

1. Preheat the oven to 200°C (400°F), Gas mark 6.

2. Knead the crushed cardamom seeds into the sweet white bun dough. Divide the dough into 12 balls and roll on a clean worktop under the palms of your hands to make round buns. Cover any dough that's waiting to be rolled with a tea towel.

3. Place the round buns spaced apart on a large baking sheet. Cover with a tea towel and leave to rise in a warm part of your kitchen for 1 hour or until almost doubled in size. When you press the dough gently, it should feel airy and the dent of your finger should remain.

4. Bake the buns for 15 minutes or until golden and hollow sounding when tapped on the base. Brush with the bun wash while still hot. Allow to cool.

5. Make the icing by mixing just enough lemon juice into the icing sugar until it is a spreadable consistency.

TIPS
It's always a help to dip a palette knife into boiling water before spreading the icing over the top of each bun.
Use a pestle and mortar to grind the whole seeds, or place in a plastic bag and crush with a rolling pin.

Banana bread with ginger and cinnamon

MAKES 1 X 900G (2LB) LOAF

I love banana bread in every shape and form. This is my current favourite, with a subtle tickling warmth coming from the ginger and cinnamon. It's the recipe we make at the cookery school which came from Darina's mother. Time to put the kettle on …

225g (8oz) plain flour
1 tsp baking powder
1 tsp ground ginger
1 tsp ground cinnamon
¼ tsp sea salt
150g (5oz) light brown sugar
375g (13oz) very ripe peeled bananas (weigh when peeled)
2 eggs

1. Preheat the oven to 180°C (350°F), Gas mark 4. Line a 900g (2lb) loaf tin with baking parchment.

2. Sift the flour, baking powder, ground ginger and cinnamon into a bowl. Mix in the salt and sugar.

3. Place the bananas on a plate and mash them well. Whisk the eggs and mix into the bananas.

4. Pour the wet ingredients into the dry ingredients and mix well – it will be sloppy.

5. Pour the mixture into the prepared tin and bake in the oven for 1hour 10 minutes or until a skewer inserted in the centre comes out clean. Turn out and allow to cool on a wire rack.

Amma's Icelandic kleinur

MAKES 30–35 TWISTS

You see versions of these delicious doughnuts all over Scandinavia and the Nordic countries. They are slightly different to American doughnuts in that they are not yeast-leavened but made with baking powder, and the dough is rolled and formed into knots before being fired. Amma used to make these, and my grandfather loved them. I never got her recipe, but this has been created in tribute to her. They're a big hit in our house.

300g (11oz) plain flour, plus extra for dusting
100g (3½oz) caster sugar
3 tsp baking powder
¾ tsp bread soda (bicarbonate of soda)
½ tsp freshly ground seeds from green cardamom pods (see tip, page 220)
50g (2oz) butter
175g (6oz) natural yoghurt
1 egg
oil (such as sunflower oil) for deep-frying
caster sugar, or caster sugar mixed with a sprinkle of ground cinnamon, for dusting

To serve
coffee or glass of milk

1. Place the flour in a bowl and add the caster sugar, baking powder, bicarbonate of soda and ground cardamom seeds. Cut the butter into cubes and rub it into the dry ingredients.

2. In a separate bowl, whisk together the yoghurt and egg. Add the wet ingredients to the dry ingredients and mix well to form a ball of dough, kneading it lightly to bring it together. Roll the ball in a little flour, then slightly flatten it, place in a plastic bag or cover with cling film and put in the fridge for 30 minutes.

3. Meanwhile, heat the oil in a deep-fat fryer or in a saucepan to 180°C (350°F).

4. Take the dough out of the fridge and roll out on a lightly floured surface until it is 3mm (⅛in) thick. You'll need to regularly dust it on top and underneath with flour to stop it sticking. It should be 45cm (17¾in) square. Trim the edges and cut into strips 6cm (2½in) wide, then cut the strips diagonally into diamonds that are 12cm (4½in) long. Take each diamond and cut a line 3cm (1¼in) long down the centre, then bring up one end of the diamond, tuck it through the hole and bring it out the other side, as shown in the picture. Now you have the Icelandic *kleinur* twist. Place the twists on a floured worktop until ready to be cooked.

5. Cook a few twists at a time in the hot oil – they'll brown quite quickly. Turn them over and cook on the other side. As soon as they're a rich golden brown, use a slotted spoon to quickly lift them out of the oil and drain on kitchen paper. Dust them with caster sugar or cinnamon sugar, just as how my grandpa loved them, before eating, as soon as they come out of the pan. Serve with coffee or a cold glass of milk.

Chocolate and almond cake with Disaronno cream

A brilliantly rich and gluten-free cake that delivers a delicious nuttiness as well as an intense chocolate hit. I love the bit of kick that comes from the Disaronno, but feel free to ring the changes with another liqueur or a small splash of vanilla extract.

100g (3½oz) butter, plus extra for greasing
150g (5oz) dark chocolate
150g (5oz) ground almonds
150g (5oz) caster sugar
pinch of sea salt
4 eggs
finely grated zest of 1 orange

For the Disaronno cream
200ml (7fl oz) whipping cream
1 tbsp icing sugar
2 tbsp Disaronno

1. Preheat the oven to 180°C (350°F), Gas mark 4. Line the base of a 20cm (8in) springform cake tin and butter the sides.

2. Place the chocolate and butter in a bowl sitting over a pan of simmering water and leave to melt. Take off the heat and set aside.

3. Place the ground almonds, caster sugar and salt in a bowl. When the chocolate and butter have cooled slightly, drop the eggs and orange zest in and whisk to mix. Pour into the dry ingredients and mix well.

4. Tip into the prepared tin and bake in the oven for 30 minutes or until a skewer inserted into the centre comes out clean. It should not feel springy in the centre but rather more fudgey. Take out of the oven and leave it in the tin for at least 10 minutes. Take out of the tin, peel off the paper and place upright again on a serving plate.

5. To make the Disaronno cream, whip the cream with the icing sugar until soft peaks form, then fold in the Disaronno and set aside in the fridge. Serve with the cake.

Gooseberry upside-down cake

SERVES 8

Anyone who knows my cooking is already aware of the fact that I'm a sucker for an upside-down cake. They're quick-and-easy to make, ultra versatile and oh-so scrummy. I'll use whatever fruit I can get my hands on to turn upside down with a cake attached. This gooseberry version is a dinger and can be made with fresh or frozen gooseberries.

50g (2oz) butter
275g (10oz) caster sugar
225g (8oz) gooseberries,
  topped and tailed
200g (7oz) plain flour
1 tsp baking powder
½ tsp sea salt
¼ tsp bread soda
  (bicarbonate of soda)
2 eggs
200ml (7fl oz) buttermilk
75ml (3fl oz) sunflower oil

To serve
brown sugar
softly whipped cream

1. You will need a 25cm (10in) diameter ovenproof, sauté or frying pan. Preheat the oven to 180°C (350°F), Gas mark 4.

2. Melt the butter in the ovenproof pan. Stir in half the sugar and cook over a gentle heat for 2 minutes. Add the gooseberries and set aside.

3. Sift the flour, baking powder, salt and bicarbonate of soda into a large bowl. Whisk the eggs in a measuring jug or small bowl, then add the remaining sugar, the buttermilk and oil and mix together. Pour this mixture into the dry ingredients and whisk to form a batter. Pour the batter over the gooseberries in the pan.

4. Place the pan in the oven and bake for 30–35 minutes until the cake feels firm in the centre. Let the cake stand for just 1 minute before turning out of the pan and onto a plate, otherwise the gooseberries will stick to the pan.

5. To turn out the cake, place an inverted plate over the top of the pan and turn the pan and plate over together in one quick movement. Lift off the pan. Serve the cake warm or at room temperature sprinkled with brown sugar, with softly whipped cream.

Chocolate birthday cake

SERVES 8

This is a great all-rounder chocolate cake that's perfect for birthday parties or just to enjoy with a cup of tea. I often make twice the recipe and cook it in two 26cm (10½in) or 28cm (11in) tins. With a selection of other birthday party treats, this would be enough cake to feed about 20.

150g (5oz) butter, softened, plus extra for greasing
200g (7oz) plain flour, plus extra for dusting
125g (4½oz) dark chocolate
3 tbsp milk
150g (5oz) caster sugar
3 eggs
1 tbsp good-quality cocoa powder
1 tsp baking powder
¼ tsp bread soda (bicarbonate of soda)

For the chocolate butter icing
150g (5oz) butter, softened
2 tbsp cream
1 tsp vanilla extract
350g (12oz) icing sugar
1 tbsp cocoa powder

To decorate
small chocolates, candy-coated chocolate beans or chocolate curls, or candles

1. Preheat the oven to 180°C (350°F), Gas mark 4. Butter and flour the sides of two 20cm (8in) sandwich tins and line the bases with baking parchment.

2. Place the chocolate and the milk in a bowl sitting over a saucepan of gently simmering water and heat until the chocolate has melted.

3. Beat the butter until very soft, then add the caster sugar and continue to beat until the mixture is light and fluffy. Beat in the eggs, one at a time, then fold in the melted chocolate.

4. Sift in the flour, cocoa powder, baking powder and the bicarbonate of soda and fold in gently to mix. Divide the mixture between the two tins and bake in the oven for 25 minutes or until a skewer inserted into the middle of each cake comes out clean.

5. Remove the cakes from the oven and leave to stand for a few minutes before turning them out of their tins and placing them on a wire rack to cool.

6. While the cakes are cooling, make the chocolate butter icing. Beat the butter, cream and the vanilla extract until very soft, then gradually sift in the icing sugar and the cocoa powder, beating all the time, until it is combined. Continue to beat until very soft, then whisk the mixture until it is light and fluffy (I often make the chocolate butter icing in an electric food mixer, using the whisk all the way through).

7. Once the cakes are cool, sandwich them together with some of the chocolate butter icing spread in between, then spread the remaining icing over the top, using a palette knife to smooth it out.

8. Transfer to a plate or cake stand and decorate the top how you wish, with small chocolates, chocolate curls or just candles.

Madeira cake

SERVES 6–8

Apart from Christmas cake, the cake I remember my mum making most was Madeira cake, which I still absolutely adore. Each of these two versions deliver an intriguing floral note. Make sure you don't overcook the cake or it will be dry.

Saffron and cardamom

pinch of saffron strands
scant ½ tsp cardamom
    seeds (from 5 fat green
    cardamom pods)
1 tbsp milk
175g (6oz) butter
175g (6oz) caster sugar
3 eggs
225g (8oz) plain flour
1 tsp baking powder

1. Preheat the oven to 170°C (325°F), Gas mark 3. Line a 900g (2lb) loaf tin with baking parchment.

2. Place the saffron and the cardamom seeds in a pestle and mortar and crush well. Tip the crushed seeds into a small saucepan, add the milk and heat up just a little. Set aside and allow to infuse.

3. In a bowl, beat the butter well until soft and light, then add the sugar and beat again. Beat in the eggs, one at a time, then sift in the flour and baking powder, add the milk and spice mixture and stir to combine.

4. Tip the mixture into the prepared loaf tin, spreading it out evenly. Bake for 50 minutes or until risen and golden, and a skewer inserted into the centre comes out clean. Leave in the tin for 5 minutes, then transfer to a wire rack to cool. Cut into slices to serve.

Pistachio and rose

175g (6oz) butter, softened
200g (7oz) caster sugar
3 eggs
1 tsp rose water
50g (2oz) pistachio nuts,
    chopped
225g (8oz) plain flour
1 tsp baking powder
2 tbsp milk

1. Preheat the oven to 170°C (325°F), Gas mark 3. Line a 900g (2lb) loaf tin with baking parchment.

2. In a bowl, beat the butter well until soft and light, then add the sugar and beat again. Beat in the eggs, one at a time, then mix in the rose water and the chopped nuts. Sift in the flour and baking powder and stir in the milk.

3. Tip the mixture into the prepared loaf tin, spreading it out evenly. Bake for 55 minutes or until a skewer inserted into the centre comes out clean. Leave in the tin for 10 minutes, then transfer to a wire rack to cool. Cut into slices to serve.

Lemon drizzle golden syrup cake

As with many of my favourite recipes, this one evolves each time I bake it. It started life as a spiced golden syrup cake, but as soon as I tasted it, I realised it was crying out for some fresh lemony zing and, hey presto, here's a delicious treat to enjoy with a cup of tea.

300g (11oz) golden syrup
150g (5oz) butter, cut into cubes
150g (5oz) caster sugar
2 eggs
300g (11oz) plain flour
1½ tsp baking powder
1½ tsp ground ginger
1½ tsp ground cinnamon
¼ tsp sea salt
1 tsp bread soda (bicarbonate of soda)
75ml (3fl oz) cooled tea

For the drizzle top
75g (3oz) caster or granulated sugar
finely grated zest and juice of 1 lemon

1. Preheat the oven to 150°C (300°F), Gas mark 2. Line the base and sides of a 20cm (8in) square tin.

2. Place the golden syrup, 200ml (7fl oz) water, the butter and the caster sugar in a saucepan and stir while the butter melts and the mixture comes to the boil. Take off the heat and set aside to cool slightly.

3. Whisk the eggs in a bowl and set aside.

4. Sift the flour, the baking powder, ginger, cinnamon and the salt into a bowl.

5. Whisk the eggs with the golden syrup mixture, then add the bicarbonate of soda into the tea, stir and pour into the egg and golden syrup mix. Add to the dry ingredients, using a whisk to mix – it will be very wet.

6. Pour into the lined tin and bake in the oven for 50–60 minutes until a skewer comes out clean when inserted into the centre.

7. While the cake is cooking, mix the ingredients for the drizzle topping in a bowl.

8. When the cake is cooked, take it out of the oven and immediately pour the drizzle over the entire top of the cake. Set aside and allow to cool. Cut into squares to serve.

Blueberry and lemon almond cake

SERVES 6–8

Sweet blueberries love the tangy kick of lemons, while lots of ground almonds bring a buttery richness to this gorgeous gluten-free cake.

100g (3½oz) butter, plus extra for greasing
100g (3½oz) caster sugar
finely grated zest of 1 lemon
2 eggs
150g (5oz) ground almonds
100g (3½oz) blueberries (fresh or frozen)
25g (1oz) fresh blueberries, to decorate

For the lemon icing
75g (3oz) icing sugar
juice of ¼ lemon

1. Preheat the oven to 170°C (325°F), Gas mark 3. Butter the sides of a 20cm (8in) cake tin (I use a springform tin) and line the base with a disc of baking parchment.

2. Cream the butter very well, then add the caster sugar and lemon zest and beat well. Then, add the eggs, one by one. Mix in the ground almonds, then tip the mixture into the prepared tin, levelling it out well. Scatter the blueberries over the top.

3. Bake in the oven for 30–35 minutes until a skewer inserted into the centre comes out clean. Take out of the oven and leave to stand for 10 minutes, then carefully transfer to a cooling rack.

4. Once cool, place the cake on a serving plate and make the lemon icing. Sift the icing sugar into a bowl and gradually mix in enough lemon juice to bring it to a thick, creamy, drizzling consistency. Drizzle the icing in a criss-cross design over the top of the cake, and then scatter with the fresh blueberries.

Lemon and liquorice cake

MAKES 16 SQUARES

My mum's favourite sweet growing up in Iceland was liquorice, and it's still a favourite of both hers and mine. It adds its own bit of magic not just to lemon, but chocolate cakes, too. Here is a recipe that combines liquorice's distinctive flavour with lemon.

200g (7oz) butter, softened
100g (3½oz) caster sugar
100g (3½oz) soft brown
   sugar
finely grated zest of 1 lemon
3 eggs
200g (7oz) plain flour
1½ tsp baking powder
2 tsp liquorice powder (see
   tip)
pinch of sea salt

For the liquorice syrup
75g (3oz) caster sugar
juice of 1 lemon
2 tbsp chopped sweet
   liquorice
2 tsp liquorice powder

1. Preheat the oven to 180°C (350°F), Gas mark 4. Line the base and the sides of a 20cm (8in) square cake tin with baking parchment.

2. Place the butter in a bowl and cream it well, then add the caster sugar, brown sugar and the lemon zest and beat until light and fluffy. Next, add the eggs, one by one, beating all the time, then sift in the flour, baking powder and liquorice powder and add the salt. As soon as it's combined, stop mixing or the cake will be tough.

3. Tip into the prepared tin and level the top with a spatula or spoon. Bake for 25–30 minutes until a skewer inserted into the centre comes out clean.

4. While the cake is cooking, make the liquorice syrup. Place the caster sugar, lemon juice, chopped sweet liquorice and liquorice powder in a saucepan and put over a medium heat. Stir while it heats up, to dissolve the sugar, then remove the spoon, turn up the heat and boil for 2 minutes until it is slightly thickened.

5. When the cake is cooked, take it out of the oven and pour the hot syrup all over the top, allowing it to soak in as the cake cools. Make sure that the chopped sweet liquorice is evenly dispersed over the top. Leave the cake to stand for a few minutes before removing it from the tin and cutting it into squares.

TIP
You can whiz up some liquorice root in a spice grinder or coffee grinder to get liquorice powder.

Chocolate and vanilla marbled pound cake

SERVES 6–8

A pound cake typically refers to a great big cake made with a pound of butter, a pound of sugar, a pound of eggs and a pound of flour, though really any cake with equal quantities of these ingredients is called a pound cake now. This is a delicious version with a generous swirling of chocolate through vanilla-scented cake.

175g (6oz) butter, softened
175g (6oz) caster sugar
3 eggs
175g (6oz) plain flour
1½ tsp baking powder
pinch of sea salt
2 tbsp milk
25g (1oz) cocoa powder, sifted
1 tsp vanilla extract

1. Preheat the oven to 180°C (350°F), Gas mark 4. Line a 900g (2lb) loaf tin with baking parchment.

2. Cream the butter in a bowl, then add the sugar and beat until light and fluffy. Add the eggs, one by one, beating well. Next, sift in the flour, baking powder and salt, then add the milk and mix gently, not beating or it will become tough.

3. Tip half the cake mixture into another bowl and fold in the sifted cocoa powder. Mix the vanilla extract into the mixture in the other bowl.

4. Place the cake mixtures into the prepared loaf tin by alternating large tablespoonfuls of each, next to and on top of each other. Using the handle of one of the spoons, draw a few swirls through the mixture to give it a lovely marbled effect.

5. Bake in the oven for 45–50 minutes until a skewer inserted into the centre comes out clean. Leave to stand in the tin for 5 minutes, then lift out and cool on a wire rack.

Upside-down toffee pineapple cake

SERVES 6–8

A nod to the early 1900s upside-down pineapple cake, but in this recipe there's not a glacé cherry in sight. It's a great upside-down cake with a delicious, sweet, caramelised pineapple topping.

For the toffee pineapple layer
75g (3oz) butter
75g (3oz) soft light brown sugar
pinch of sea salt
350g (12oz) pineapple, cut into 1cm/½in chunks

For the cake layer
150g (5oz) plain flour
1½ tsp baking powder
¼ tsp sea salt
3 eggs
150g (5oz) butter, melted
150g (5oz) soft light brown sugar
1 tsp finely grated lemon zest

1. You will need a 23cm (9in) ovenproof sauté or frying pan. Preheat the oven to 180°C (350°F), Gas mark 4.

2. Start with the toffee pineapple layer. Place the pan over a medium heat, add the butter and allow it to melt, then stir in the sugar, salt and chopped pineapple. Cook, uncovered, over the medium heat for 10 minutes, stirring regularly, or until the pineapple is tender and coated in a rich golden toffee sauce. The pineapple should evenly cover the floor of the pan.

3. Next, make the cake layer. Sift the flour and baking powder into a bowl and mix in the salt. In another bowl, whisk the eggs with the melted butter, then mix in the sugar and lemon zest. Make a well in the centre of the dry ingredients, pour in the egg mixture and, using a whisk, bring it together until just combined.

4. Pour it carefully and evenly over the pineapple in the pan, so as not to disturb the pineapple. It should completely cover it.

5. Bake in the oven for 22–25 minutes until a skewer inserted into the centre comes out clean.

6. Place a serving plate over the top of the pan and carefully flip both plate and pan over so that the cake is sitting pineapple-side up. Allow to cool, then serve.

Iced banoffee cake

SERVES 6

If the banana-toffee twosome is your thing, then try making this version of a banoffee cake that can conveniently be made ahead and stored in the freezer until serving.

3 bananas
800ml (1 pint 9fl oz) vanilla ice cream, slightly softened
grated chocolate, to serve

For the base
200g (7oz) digestive biscuits
75g (3oz) butter, melted

For the toffee sauce
75g (3oz) butter
50g (2oz) brown sugar
90g (3½oz) golden syrup
30g (1¼oz) plain flour
75ml (3fl oz) regular or double cream
75ml (3fl oz) milk

1. Put the base of a 23cm (9in) springform cake tin upside down in the tin (so that the lip of the base is facing down) and secure the clasp. This will make it easier to slide the cake off the tin base when it's ready to serve.

2. Put the biscuits in the bowl of a food processor and whiz to the consistency of coarse breadcrumbs (or place in a plastic bag and bash with a rolling pin). Tip them out into a bowl, add the melted butter and mix well, then tip into the tin. Press firmly into the bottom of the tin to create an even layer, then flatten the surface and place in the fridge while you make the toffee sauce.

3. Melt the butter in a saucepan over a medium heat. Add the brown sugar and golden syrup and bring to the boil, then add the flour and whisk the mixture over the heat until it is smooth and thickened. Next, pour in the cream and milk, whisking all the time, and continue to boil, while whisking, for another 2 minutes until thickened. Take off the heat and set aside to cool slightly.

4. Peel the bananas and cut into slices 5mm (¼in) thick, then lay evenly over the biscuit base. Once the sauce has almost cooled, pour it over the bananas. Place in the freezer for 5–10 minutes and take out the ice cream to soften slightly. Spread the slightly softened ice cream over the toffee sauce to cover it completely, then return to the freezer until the ice cream is firm.

5. When ready to serve, scatter the cake with the grated chocolate and cut into slices. Serve straightaway.

Apple fudge cake

Apples love toffee, and in this delicious and easy-to-put-together cake they make a super pair, giving you a lovely treat to have with a cup of coffee or at the end of a meal.

3 eating apples, peeled,
    quartered and cored
50g (2oz) butter
75g (3oz) brown sugar

For the cake batter
125g (4½oz) butter
125g (4½oz) brown sugar
3 eggs
125g (4½oz) plain flour
1 tsp baking powder
1 tbsp milk

For the toffee sauce
110g (4oz) butter, diced
250g (9oz) brown sugar
275g (10oz) golden syrup
225ml (8fl oz) regular or
    double cream
1 tsp vanilla extract

1. Preheat the oven to 180°C (350°F), Gas mark 4. Cut each apple quarter lengthways in half and set aside for a moment.

2. Melt the butter in an ovenproof frying pan or a 20cm (8in) sauté pan over a medium heat. Add the sugar and stir over the heat for a few seconds, making sure it's evenly distributed on the floor of the pan. Take the pan off the heat and arrange the apples in a single layer in the pan (this will be the top of the cake when it's cooked, so arrange them with this in mind).

3. To make the batter, cream the butter well, then add the sugar, mixing all the time. When it's soft and light, add the eggs, one at a time, then sift in the flour and baking powder and mix gently. Stir in the milk. (Or, if you like, you can place all the cake batter ingredients into a food processor and whiz briefly to combine.) Pour the batter over the apples, trying not to disturb their arrangement.

4. Place in the oven and bake for 40–45 minutes until the cake is spongy in the centre and a skewer inserted into the centre comes out clean. Leave to cool for a minute.

5. While the cake is baking, make the toffee sauce. Place all the ingredients in a saucepan over a medium heat. Stir until the butter has melted and the sugar dissolves. Bring to the boil and cook for 2–3 minutes, stirring regularly, until thickened and smooth. Take off the heat until you are ready to serve.

6. Slide a small sharp knife around the sides of the cake to ensure the cake is not stuck, then carefully place a plate over the top of the tin, turn the tin upside down and turn the cake out. Serve with the warmed toffee sauce.

Coconut and raspberry cake

SERVES 8–10

A delicious, simple celebratory cake that uses the classic coconut and raspberry combo to perfection.

200g (7oz) butter, plus extra for greasing
250g (9oz) plain flour, plus extra for dusting
200g (7oz) caster sugar
4 eggs
1½ tsp baking powder
50g (2oz) desiccated coconut, plus 2 tbsp
2 tbsp milk
150g (5oz) raspberry jam (see page 176 for my recipe)
150ml (5fl oz) whipping cream
icing sugar, for dusting

1. You will need 2 x 20cm (8in) round cake tins (at least 3cm/1¼in deep). Line the base with baking parchment, then butter and flour the sides of the tins. Preheat the oven to 180°C (350°F), Gas mark 4.

2. Place the butter in a bowl and beat well until soft. Beat in the sugar, then the eggs, one by one. Sift in the flour and baking powder and tip in the 50g (2oz)of coconut. Stir well, then mix in the milk to loosen. Take 3 generous tablespoons of the cake mixture and spread out in the bottom of one cake tin, then repeat with the other tin.

3. Divide the raspberry jam evenly between the tins, dotting it all over and, then, using the back of a spoon, spread it out to cover the cake mixture. Next, divide the remaining cake mixture between the tins, spreading carefully so as not to disturb the raspberry jam. Scatter 1 tablespoon desiccated coconut over each cake.

4. Bake in the oven for 30–35 minutes until golden and a skewer inserted into the centre of each cake comes out clean.

5. Remove from the oven and allow to stand for 5 minutes, then take out of the cake tins and transfer to a wire rack to cool. When cool, sandwich together with whipped cream, dust with icing sugar and serve.

Raspberry buns

A great recipe from my friend Nessa's mum, Margaret, that I found while looking through her two-generations-old handwritten cookbook. These are a combination of biscuits and scones with a sweet, tangy raspberry jam in the middle – see page 176 for my jam recipe. Perfect with a cup of tea.

350g (12oz) plain flour, plus extra for dusting
1½ tsp baking powder
75g (3oz) caster sugar
150g (5oz) butter, cut into cubes
3 eggs
50ml (2fl oz) milk
8 generous tsp raspberry jam
2 tbsp granulated sugar (or caster)

1. Preheat the oven to 200°C (400°F), Gas mark 6.

2. Sift the flour and baking powder into a bowl. Add the caster sugar, then rub in the butter. In another bowl, whisk 2 of the eggs with the milk. Make a well in the centre of the dry ingredients and pour in the egg mixture. Using a wooden spoon or your hand, bring it to a soft dough, stopping mixing once it comes together.

3. Tip the dough out onto a floured work surface. With floured hands, shape the dough into a log shape 7.5cm (3in) in diameter. Cut the log in half, then each half in half again so that you have four pieces. Again, cut each piece in half, then in half again so that you have 16 pieces, each one being roughly in a round 7cm (2¾in) in diameter. You might need to reshape them slightly with your hands. These will be the lids and bottoms of the buns.

4. Lay 8 of these rounds on your worktop, make a slight indent or hollow in the centre of each and spoon a generous teaspoon of raspberry jam into each hollow. Beat the remaining egg and place the sugar on a plate or saucer. Brush a little eggwash around the edges of each round. Top each one with a dough lid, pressing down around the edges so that they stick, and pinch the edges together to form a nice round shape. Brush the tops with beaten egg, then dip them in the sugar. Place, sugar side up, on a baking sheet, spaced slightly apart, and bake in the oven for 12–15 minutes until golden on top and underneath.

Swiss roll

A Swiss roll was one of the first cakes that my mum taught me how to bake, and it's still one of my favourites today. Soft, light sponge with a crisp sugar coating wrapped around sweet raspberry jam (page 176) – simple and completely delicious.

a little melted butter
125g (4½oz) plain flour, plus extra for dusting
4 eggs
125g (4½oz) caster sugar, plus 3 tbsp for sprinkling
1 tsp vanilla extract

For the filling
6 tbsp raspberry or strawberry jam
200ml (7fl oz) whipped cream (optional)

1. Preheat the oven to 190°C (375°F), Gas mark 5. Line the base of a 25 x 38cm (10 x 15in) Swiss roll tin with baking parchment, brush the base and sides of the tin with melted butter and dust with flour.

2. Whisk the eggs and caster sugar together in a large bowl or in an electric food mixer until light and fluffy, then add 2 tablespoons warm water and the vanilla extract. Sift in the flour, about one-third at a time, and fold it into the mixture using a large metal spoon.

3. Pour the mixture gently into the prepared Swiss roll tin and bake in the oven for 12–15 minutes until the centre of the cake is slightly springy and the edges have shrunk a little from the sides of the tin.

4. Scatter the top of the sponge with the 3 tablespoons caster sugar (this stops the roll from sticking to the paper), then place a piece of baking parchment, larger than the tin, over the top and turn out onto the paper in one quick move. Remove the tin and baking parchment from the bottom of the cake. Place a slightly damp, clean tea towel over the cake and leave to cool – this will prevent it drying out and cracking when you roll it.

5. When the cake is cool, spread it with jam, followed by the whipped cream (if you like). With the longest side facing you, roll up the Swiss roll away from you, then transfer to a plate to serve.

Retro chocolate peppermint bars

MAKES ABOUT 24 BARS

These are called 'retro' because this is a flavour that so reminds me of when my sister and I used to experiment with lots of baking when we were little. I was slightly obsessed with the chocolate-peppermint combination and made everything from cakes, buns and biscuits to petits fours and ice cream with these two ingredients. These are a mint-choc version of a millionaire's shortbread. Delicious.

For the shortbread base
300g (11oz) plain flour
100g (3½oz) sugar
200g (7oz) butter, in cubes
  (soft if possible)

For the peppermint butter filling
100g (3½oz) butter, softened
400g (14oz) icing sugar
2 tbsp milk
2 tsp peppermint essence

For the chocolate topping
200g (7oz) dark chocolate,
  or 150g (5oz) milk
  chocolate and 50g (2oz)
  dark chocolate
10g (¼oz) butter

1. You will need a small Swiss roll tin 20 x 30cm (8 x 12in) or 33 x 23cm (13 x 9in). Preheat the oven to 180°C (350°F), Gas mark 4.

2. First, make the shortbread base. Place the flour and sugar in a bowl and rub in the cubed butter. Bring the mixture together with your hands – or use a hand-held electric beater or food processor, if you like – even if it is a little crumbly. Press evenly into the Swiss roll tin and bake for 20–25 minutes until golden all over. Take out of the oven and leave to cool completely.

3. While it is cooling, make the peppermint butter filling. Cream the butter well, then add the icing sugar, milk and peppermint essence, using a hand-held electric beater or food processor, if you like.

4. When the shortbread base has cooled completely, spread the peppermint butter filling over it, using a palette knife regularly dipped in boiling water to help you. Place the tin in the fridge to chill for 30 minutes.

5. Meanwhile, put the chocolate and butter in a bowl set over a saucepan of simmering water. Once the water boils, take off the heat and set aside until the chocolate has melted, then leave to cool a little.

6. When the peppermint butter filling has cooled and set, take it out of the fridge and spread the chocolate (make sure it's not hot or it will melt the peppermint butter filling) over the top. Allow to set, then cut into bars.

Custard creams

These are what they say on the tin, but they are a really good buttery, crumbly version of those that you get in a packet.

200g (7oz) soft butter
150g (5oz) caster sugar
1 tsp vanilla extract
200g (7oz) plain flour, plus
   extra for dusting
100g (3½oz) custard powder

For the butter icing
125g (4½oz) soft butter
1 tsp vanilla extract
250g (9oz) icing sugar

1. Preheat the oven to 180°C (350°F), Gas mark 4. Line 2 or 3 baking sheets with baking parchment. Place the butter in a bowl, or in the bowl of an electric food mixer, and cream well. Add the sugar and the vanilla and beat again until soft and light. Sift in the flour and the custard powder and mix well until the dough comes together.

2. When the dough has come together, roll it out on a floured worktop with some flour dusted on top, to stop it sticking, until it is 5mm (¼in) thick. You'll probably need to regularly slide a palette knife under the dough with some flour to stop it sticking. Cut into shapes, squares or rectangles (making sure you have doubles of each shape so that they can be sandwiched together) and carefully lift onto the prepared baking sheets, spaced a little apart as they will spread ever so slightly when baking.

3. Bake in the oven for 10–15 minutes until just feeling dry around the edges and light golden in colour. Take out of the oven and leave to stand on the baking sheet for a few minutes before lifting off to cool on a wire rack.

4. While the biscuits are cooking or cooling, make the butter icing. Cream the butter and the vanilla extract in a bowl with a wooden spoon, or in the bowl of an electric mixer with the paddle attachment, and mix in the icing sugar until it comes together.

5. When the biscuits are cooked and cooled, spread some butter icing onto a biscuit then place another on top to sandwich them together. Repeat with all the others.

Lemon coconut bars

MAKES ABOUT 24 BARS

I'm a big fan of the traybake. This is a version using one of my favourite flavour combinations: tangy lemon with sweet, tropical coconut sitting over a buttery biscuit base.

For the base
125g (4½oz) butter, softened
75g (3oz) icing sugar
175g (6oz) plain flour

For the topping
4 eggs
350g (12oz) caster sugar
finely grated zest of 1 lemon
1 tsp baking powder
100ml (3½fl oz) lemon juice
60g (2½oz) desiccated
   coconut

1. First, make the shortbread base. Beat the butter well then add the icing sugar and beat to combine. Add the flour and bring together to form a dough. Spread out to cover the base of a 33 x 23cm (13 x 9in) Swiss roll tin and bake in the oven for 15–20 minutes or until golden. Take out of the oven.

2. Meanwhile, make the lemon and coconut topping. Place the eggs, caster sugar, lemon zest, baking powder and lemon juice in a bowl and whisk very well to combine thoroughly. Pour the mixture into the tin (it will be quite a thin liquid) and evenly scatter coconut over the top. Place carefully in the oven (so it doesn't spill) and cook for 20–25 minutes until golden brown and set. Take out of the oven and allow to cool in the tin.

3. Once cool, cut into bars to serve.

Almond fingers

I was telling my friend Nessa's mum, Margaret, about this cookbook that I was writing and she very kindly offered to show me her little notebook where she keeps some recipes. The next time I saw her she had in her hand a small leatherbound notebook that was only just being held together by threads from decades of use. It contained probably a hundred recipes that had been handwritten by her mother and grandmother, with Margaret's own notes and recipes jotted down in between. What a precious heirloom that book is. Here's one of the recipes from it. Thanks, Margaret.

75g (3oz) butter, cubed, plus a little melted butter for brushing the tin
175g (6oz) plain flour, plus extra for dusting
50g (2oz) caster sugar
½ tsp baking powder
1 egg, separated
50ml (2fl oz) milk
1 tsp vanilla extract
4 tbsp sieved apricot jam
50g (2oz) icing sugar
a few drops of almond essence
25g (1oz) flaked almonds

1. Preheat the oven to 180°C (350°F), Gas mark 4. Brush all over the inside of a 20 x 30cm (8 x 12in) Swiss roll tin with a little melted butter. Or you can line the tin with baking parchment, if you prefer.

2. Place the flour, sugar and baking powder in a bowl and whisk to mix. Rub the butter into the dry ingredients. Place the egg yolk in a small bowl. Add the milk and vanilla extract and whisk to mix. Pour the wet ingredients into the dry ingredients and mix to a dough.

3. Tip the dough out onto a floured work surface, dust with a little flour and roll out to a rectangle to fit the prepared tin. Transfer to the tin and smooth out so that it is evenly spread in the bottom of the tin. Spread the apricot jam evenly over the dough.

4. Place the egg white in a bowl and whisk until frothy. Sift in the icing sugar and add the almond essence, then spread thinly over the jam. It will be quite sloppy. Scatter the flaked almonds over the top.

5. Bake in the oven for 20–25 minutes until golden brown all over.

6. Take out of the oven and allow to cool for a few minutes, then cut into fingers to serve.

Preserving

Rhubarb and ginger jam

MAKES 8 X 450G (1LB) JARS

2kg (4¼lb) rhubarb
2kg (4¼lb) granulated sugar
grated zest and juice of
   2 (preferably unwaxed)
   lemons
25–50g (1–2oz) fresh ginger,
   to taste, peeled and
   bruised (bashed with a
   rolling pin)
50g (2oz) preserved ginger
   in syrup, drained and
   chopped (optional)

1. Wipe the rhubarb clean and cut into 2–3cm pieces. Place them in a large saucepan over a medium-low heat with the sugar, lemon zest and juice and the bruised ginger. Stir all the time until the sugar is dissolved, then boil rapidly until the jam sets, which takes about 10 minutes (see tip). Stir in the chopped stem ginger (if using) at the end of the cooking time.

2. Remove the piece of bruised ginger and then pour the jam into hot, clean, sterilised jars (see tip) and cover, label and store.

TIPS
To sterilise the jars, either boil them in a saucepan of water for 5 minutes, put them through a dishwasher cycle, or place them, lying on their sides, in an oven preheated to 110°C (225°F), Gas mark ¼ for 10 minutes. To sterilise the lids, put them in a pot of simmering water for 5 minutes.

To test if a jam or marmalade is ready, if you don't own a thermometer, place a small plate in the freezer for a few minutes to chill before you start making the jam. Put a small blob on the cold saucer and leave for a few seconds (the pan of jam can be off the heat at this stage). Push your finger through the blob. If it wrinkles (if a skin has formed) as you push it, it has set. If not, return the pan to the heat, cook a little longer and test again.

Gooseberry jam

MAKES 6 X 450G (1LB) JARS

1.3kg (3lb) green
   gooseberries, topped
   and tailed
5 elderflower heads
   (optional)
1.6kg (3½lb) granulated
   sugar

1. Place the gooseberries in a wide stainless-steel saucepan with 600ml (1 pint) water. If you are using the elderflower heads, tie them in a piece of muslin cloth and place in the pan. Place the pan over a medium heat and bring to a simmer, stirring regularly, then continue to simmer until the gooseberries are completely soft and have burst and the mixture has reduced by a third, for 30 minutes.

2. Remove the elderflowers (if using) and discard. Add the sugar and stir until it has completely dissolved. Increase the heat to high and boil rapidly for 10 minutes, then test it to see if the jam has set (see tip above). Pour into hot sterilised jars (see tip above) and put the lids on while still hot. The jam will keep for a few months.

Strawberry and rhubarb jam

MAKES 3 X 450G (1LB) JARS

Rhubarb and strawberry is one of the best fruit combinations, and happily nature arranged this marriage so that they're in season at the same time. My mum often made rhubarb jam and this recipe is a twist on hers, just with the addition of strawberries. You can use frozen fruit if you wish.

500g (1lb 2oz) sugar
300g (11oz) hulled and quartered strawberries (fresh or frozen)
300g (11oz) rhubarb (fresh or frozen), cut into 1cm (½in) chunks
juice of 2 lemons

1. Place the sugar in a bowl in an oven preheated to 150°C (300°F), Gas mark 2. Put a side plate in the freezer.

2. Place the strawberry and rhubarb chunks in a saucepan, a large one if possible. Put over a medium heat and mash the fruit in the pan while it's heating. As it gets hot, it will become very juicy. When it's mashed and juicy, add the lemon juice and the warmed sugar. Stir it straight away to dissolve the sugar and turn the heat up to high. Boil it while stirring regularly to stop it sticking and burning, for 6–8 minutes, depending on the size of your pan. If you're using a large saucepan, cook it for just 6 minutes.

3. Take the plate out of the freezer and test to see if the jam is set (see tip opposite).

4. Once cooked, using a spoon, skim off any of the frothy white 'scum' that is floating on top. Pour the jam into sterilised jars (see tip opposite), cover with lids and allow to cool and set. Store in a cool, dark place, like a cupboard, away from direct heat. It will keep for a few months if stored correctly in sterilised jars.

Lemon marmalade

MAKES ABOUT 3.6KG (8LB)

Tiffany and Jasper's mum Julia's marmalade is legendary. I can remember going to stay with Julia in London and she had just arrived back from the market with a basket full of wonderful-looking unwaxed lemons from Sorrento, in Italy. When I was going home after the weekend, I was thrilled to find a jar of this famous marmalade sitting on top of my suitcase. Thanks, Julia. Use the best organic unwaxed (if possible) lemons you can.

1.3kg (3lb) unwaxed lemons
1.8kg (4lb) granulated
  sugar

1. Scrub the lemons in very hot water. Cut them in half and squeeze out the juice. Set aside. Cut the lemon halves into quarters and place in a saucepan with 2.2 litres (3¾ pints) water, bring to the boil then cook for 2 hours or until they are very tender. While the lemons are cooking, place an upturned saucepan lid on top of them to keep them completely submerged.

2. When the lemons are tender, preheat the oven to 200°C (400°F), Gas mark 6. Put the sugar on a baking sheet and heat in the oven for 10 minutes.

3. Using a slotted spoon, remove the lemons from the pan. Keep the water in the pan. When cool enough to handle, shred the lemon peel and discard the pips.

4. Add the reserved lemon juice to the cooking water to make up to 1.75 litres (3 pints). Put the fruit and the liquid into a large shallow stainless-steel saucepan and bring to the boil. Add the warm sugar to the pan and stir until dissolved, then boil for 15 minutes until it sets (see tips, page 254).

5. Pour the jam into sterilised jars (see tips, page 254) and leave to stand for 10 minutes, then cover with lids, label and store.

Mint and apple jelly

MAKES ABOUT 3 X 400G (14OZ) JARS

An apple jelly is a wonderful preserve. Enjoy it on toast, pancakes or crumpets and serve with roasted pork or lamb. I love to flavour it with different herbs such as mint, lemon verbena or sweet geranium leaves, or spices like cloves, cinnamon and ginger.

1.3kg (3lb) cooking apples, washed and quartered (don't remove the peel or cores)
4 large mint sprigs
2 lemons
granulated sugar, as needed for quantity of juice
4 tbsp mint, chopped

1. Place the apples and mint sprigs in a large saucepan with 1.3 litres (2¼pints) water. Use a peeler to peel the rind from the two lemons (reserving the lemons for later) and add to the pan. Place over a medium heat and cook, uncovered, stirring occasionally, for 45 minutes or until reduced to a pulp.

2. Allow to cool slightly, then pour into a jelly bag or a large piece of muslin sitting in a large nylon sieve. If using muslin, you can tie a knot in it once the apple mixture is all in and hang it up on a hook so that the juice from it drips into the bowl below; you won't need the sieve. The jelly bag can be hung on a hook or something similar over a bowl, too. Allow to drip through until all the juice has been extracted – usually a few hours or even overnight if you want to get every bit out of it. For a clear glossy jelly, do not push the mixture through to speed it up.

3. Next, measure the apple juice into a large saucepan and allow 500g (1lb 2oz) sugar for each 500ml (18fl oz) juice, placing the weighed sugar in a bowl to warm up in an oven preheated to 150°C (300°F), Gas mark 2. Place a small plate or saucer in the freezer.

4. Squeeze the reserved lemons, strain the juice and add to the saucepan. Place over a high heat and bring to the boil with the extracted apple juice, then add the warmed sugar. Stir together until the sugar is dissolved, then boil rapidly, uncovered, for 10 minutes.

5. Next, remove the plate from the freezer and use to test the set of the jelly (see tips page 254).

6. Skim any scum that has risen to the top and stir through the chopped mint. Immediately pour into sterilised jars (see tips page 254), then cover and set aside to cool and set. Store in a cool dark place away from direct heat. It will keep for a few months.

Caulikraut

This very simple fermented vegetable recipe comes from my sister-in-law Penny. It can add heaps of beneficial bacteria into your diet and is her daughter India's favourite thing to eat right now. The most important thing to know for successfully preserving vegetables in this way is to make sure that everything is submerged under the liquid. Penny cleverly keeps a selection of small jars to use as weights that fit into the top of the fermenting jar.

1 small head of cauliflower, preferably organic
4 tsp sea salt
1 red onion (or white – red gives a lovely pink tinge to the finished ferment), thinly sliced
1 garlic clove, finely chopped
juice of 1 orange

1. Break the cauliflower into florets and then slice each floret as thinly as possible. Place in a mixing bowl.

2. Add the sea salt to the cauliflower and mix well with your hands. The salt will start to draw water out of the vegetable – this is what you want, this brine is going to cover the vegetables and keep the air out for successful fermentation to take place.

3. Add the onion and garlic to the cauliflower along with the orange juice and mix well again.

4. Take handfuls of the mixture and pack it into a 1 litre (1¾ pint) clip-top jar or similar. Push each handful down tightly with your fist until it's all in. Place a small, clean jam jar on top of the vegetables and secure the clip-top lid over it – this will keep the vegetables submerged under the brine. If there's not enough brine to cover everything, add a tablespoon or two of water.

5. Leave it out of the fridge on a countertop with a plate underneath (to catch drips if it gets very bubbly) for a week to 10 days. You will start to see lots of bubbles after about three days – this is the beneficial bacteria working away. Taste it after seven days, it should taste pleasantly sour. Store it in the fridge once it's to your liking – where it will keep for several months – and enjoy.

Apple and tomato chutney

It's such a treat to have preserves in the cupboard to enjoy all year round. We normally have a glut of apples that need using in the autumn time. I eat this delicious chutney with everything from cheese and cold meats to sausages and shepherd's pie.

2 large cooking apples, peeled, cored and roughly chopped
500g (1lb 2oz) ripe red tomatoes, peeled and chopped (see tip, page 114)
2 onions, finely chopped
300g (11oz) light brown sugar
225ml (8fl oz) cider vinegar
110g (4oz) sultanas
2 tsp salt
½ tsp ground ginger
½ tsp freshly ground black pepper
¼ tsp cayenne pepper
¼ tsp ground cinnamon
¼ tsp ground allspice

1. Place all the ingredients in a stainless-steel saucepan, over a medium-high heat and bring to the boil, stirring to dissolve the sugar. Continue to lightly boil, uncovered, turning the heat down if it's starting to 'spit', stirring regularly to make sure the bottom doesn't burn, for 1 hour or until it is thick and pulpy.

2. Pour into hot, sterilised jars (see tips, page 254) and cover while the chutney is still hot. When cool, label and store in a cool dark place, like a cupboard, away from direct heat. It will keep for a few months.

Piccalilli

MAKES 4 X 400G (14OZ) JARS

Piccalilli always reminds me of my mum. I love a quick snack of cheese on Scandi crackers with sweet, sharp and crunchy piccalilli, just like I remember my mum doing when we were young.

If you don't have all the vegetables listed don't worry, just add extra of something, as long as the final weight is 750g (1lb 10oz)

60g (2½oz) cauliflower, cut into 1cm (½in) florets

60g (2½oz) broccoli, cut into 1cm (½in) florets

60g (2½oz) peas (frozen are fine)

60g (2½oz) shallots, cut into even 5mm (¼in) dice

60g French beans, cut into 1cm (½in) pieces

60g (2½oz) carrot, cut into 1cm (½in) dice

60g (2½oz) sweetcorn kernels

60g (2½oz) celery, cut into 1cm (½in) dice

70g (2½oz) red pepper, deseeded and cut into 1cm (½in) dice

100g (3½oz) tomato, peeled, deseeded and cut into 1cm (½in) dice (see tip, page 114)

100g (3½oz) apple, peeled, cored and cut into 1cm (½in) dice

50g (2oz) salt dissolved in 500ml (18fl oz) cold water (as cold as possible)

2 tsp sunflower oil

1. Place the prepared vegetables in a bowl, cover with the salt water, toss well and leave in the fridge for at least 1 hour.

2. Warm the sunflower oil in a pot large enough to hold all the ingredients. Add the coriander, fennel, cumin, turmeric, chilli and nutmeg, and lightly fry for a few minutes, but don't allow to darken or burn. Add the vinegar and honey and bring to a bubble.

3. Drain the vegetables and rinse well under cold running water, then drain again very well. Add the vegetables to the pot with the spices, vinegar and honey and bring to a boil. Dissolve the cornflour in 100ml (3½fl oz) water in a small bowl or cup and add to the pot, then continue boiling, stirring well, for 2 minutes or until it thickens.

4. Using a jam funnel, fill four hot sterilised jars (see tips, page 254) with piccalilli, then cover with the hot sterilised lids. Allow to cool, then label and store in a dark cupboard, or in the fridge once opened.

TIP
To toast the spices, put the whole seeds in a dry pan over a medium heat, shaking regularly until they start to darken and release a good aroma. Transfer while still warm to a spice grinder or to a pestle and mortar and grind.

1 tsp coriander seeds,
   toasted and ground
   (see tip)
1 tsp fennel seeds, toasted
   and ground (see tip)
1 tsp cumin seeds, toasted
   and ground (see tip)
2 tsp ground turmeric
¼ tsp dried chilli flakes
½ tsp grated nutmeg
250ml (9fl oz) cider vinegar
150g (5oz) honey
25g (1oz) cornflour

Mum with a friend (above), and camping with Amma and Kristin (below).

Sloe gin

MAKES 560ML (1 PINT)

Another go-to recipe from Tiffany's mum Julia and a great excuse for a forage. Look out for sloes in hedgerows – once you find a good crop, make sure they are firm, not too hard and not too squishy, as they would make the gin pulpy (they must keep their shape when you prick them with a pin).

225g (8oz) sloes, pricked (see tips)
600ml (1 pint) gin
115g (4oz) caster sugar
12 blanched, bruised (bashed with a rolling pin) almonds

1. Sterilise the bottles (see tips, page 254). You can jiggle quantities to fit the bottles, but if you have them, 2 litre (3½ pint) bottles work well for the above quantities.

2. Divide the ingredients between the bottles, then plug each one with an airtight stopper.

3. Turn and gently shake the bottles daily for the first week to help it along, then store somewhere dark, preferably under lock and key! Try to wait a month, ideally longer, before enjoying a drop.

4. Drink straight in dinky glasses. Alternatively, at cocktail hour serve as sloe gin and tonics; or add a splash of hot water to warm your cockles in winter

TIPS
Sloes are the berry of the blackthorn and there are lots of tips online as to where to forage for them. You're meant to wait until the first frost before picking, but go with what your fingers tell you. Last year we picked in October, way before the first frost. We had to wrestle with the birds, who love this berry. Make sure to pierce each sloe a couple of times using a needle or cocktail stick.

Elderflower cordial

MAKES 2 LITRES (3½ PINTS)

When I asked my friend Tiffany which of her mum's recipes was her favourite, the first one she said was elderflower cordial. The pretty white flowers of the elder tree that bloom in May and June have an intriguing flavour that comes alive when mixed with sugar and lemon. This cordial is, of course, great diluted with water, but also delicious with sparkling water or wine, and wickedly delicious in a gin and tonic.

1.6kg (3½lb) caster or
    granulated sugar
3 lemons, thinly sliced
25 elderflower heads
50g (2oz) citric acid

1. Place the sugar and 1 litre (1¾ pints) water in a saucepan over a high heat and bring to the boil while stirring to dissolve the sugar. Boil for 1 minute, then set aside to cool.

2. Place the lemons in a bowl. Add the elderflowers and the citric acid. Pour over the cool syrup and stir to mix.

3. Leave to stand for two to three days at room temperature, then strain through a jelly bag or some muslin that you've placed in a sieve. Decant into sterilised bottles (see tips, page 254) and store in a cool, dark place, or in the fridge. It will keep for a few months.

Index

Acknowledgements

Thank you and big hugs again to all my friends and family for giving me delicious recipes, constant support and lots of love. A particularly huge hug and thanks to my husband Zac, who works with me on everything I do. And our great friend, my cousin-in-law, Ivan Whelan for being so wonderful and such great company while we tested the recipes for this book. Huge thanks as well to Darina, Timmy, Rory and everyone at Ballymaloe – I count myself so lucky to be surrounded by the most amazing team of people at the Ballymaloe Cookery School. You are all fabulous. And thank you to Brian Walsh at RTE for all the support over the years.

I must also thank, as always, all the people who work so hard putting my books together. Grace Cheetham and Georgina Mackenzie for their support, guidance and editorial nous. Hannah Gamon and Isabel Prodger for their Marketing and Publicity expertise. James Empringham for his (as ever) wonderful art direction and design flair. And I've really loved working with Zoe Berville who helped hugely to get this project over the finish line. Thanks again to the brilliant Maja Smend and her assistant Sam Folan for taking such beautiful images. To Annie Rigg for preparing and styling the food so beautifully on the shoot and Lydia Brun who has such a wonderful eye for props. Thank you also to Liz McCarthy for your fab make-up artistry. To Fiona Lindsay and her team at Limelight Management, big hugs and thanks for your enduring support. And finally, thanks to all the wonderful people who buy my books; for your feedback and for your friendly hellos when I'm out and about.